Quarterly Essay

Quarterly Essay is published four times a year by Black Inc., an imprint of Schwartz Publishing Pty Ltd. Publisher: Morry Schwartz.

ISBN 9781760640705 ISSN 1832-0953

Subscriptions – 1 year print & digital (4 issues): $79.95 within Australia incl. GST. Outside Australia $119.95. 2 years print & digital (8 issues): $149.95 within Australia incl. GST. 1 year digital only: $49.95.

Payment may be made by Mastercard or Visa, or by cheque made out to Schwartz Publishing. Payment includes postage and handling.

To subscribe, fill out and post the subscription card or form inside this issue, or subscribe online:

quarterlyessay.com
subscribe@blackincbooks.com
Phone: 61 3 9486 0288

Correspondence should be addressed to:

The Editor, Quarterly Essay
Level 1, 221 Drummond Street
Carlton VIC 3053 Australia
Phone: 61 3 9486 0288 / Fax: 61 3 9011 6106
Email: quarterlyessay@blackincbooks.com

Editor: Chris Feik. Management: Caitlin Yates. Publicity: Anna Lensky. Design: Guy Mirabella. Assistant Editor: Kirstie Innes- Will. Production Coordinator: Hanako Smith. Typesetting: Akiko Chan.

FOLLOW THE LEADER

Democracy and the Rise of the Strongman

Laura Tingle

London, June 2017. A leadership crisis is upon us. Having cheerfully followed my lead as we clambered over the remnants of ancient Roman civilisation at the beginning of my first Quarterly Essay, *Great Expectations*, and contemplated Tacitus and the fall of the Roman Empire at the beginning of my second, *Political Amnesia*, Tosca Ramsey, my daughter, my *diva filia*, has had enough as we travel on perhaps our last Excellent Girls' Adventure abroad together. Now almost nineteen, Tosca has perfected the teenage eye-roll and barely disguised contempt. "Oh. My. God," Tosca says, as I prod helplessly at a ticket machine in the vast concourse of Waterloo Station. "I can't believe you just did that." She strides off to sort out our ticket purchases, gloriously unaware of the young men walking into poles and garbage bins as she passes by. Although oblivious to the path of male destruction she leaves in her wake, she is more than aware of the effect she is having on her mother: the assertion of independence; of greater knowledge of the world and what is needed to operate in it; of greater competence and capacity to lead us on the next stage of our journey. Happy to follow along on our past adventures, in this one my girl has nicked the field marshal's baton from my knapsack and made a charge for the front.

Leadership, it turns out, is a two-way thing. Leaders kid themselves that they are setting the terms of play, even running the world. And we write and think about them in those terms. But in fact true leaders only get to lead if they have followers whom they can persuade to follow. So often it is what followers want that determines whether leaders get to emerge at all. And as we have seen in Australia in recent years, it is followers in the party – and what they *think* followers outside the party – want that determines whether they stay there.

I didn't yet realise, when I was being bathed in scorn at Waterloo Station, that there was an obvious final instalment, a trilogy to complete, in the consideration of Australian expectations of government, and our failing institutional memory, that I began in 2012. That final instalment concerns political leadership in the modern world. For whatever our expectations of government, whatever the state of our institutions and institutional memory, it is leadership that helps both to settle those things, and change them.

We don't much discuss our expectations of government, or consider the changing nature of the institutions that hold our society together, and so often we have faulty memories of what has gone before. But we do increasingly focus our frustration with our society and our politics on the human form of our leaders. We bemoan a lack of leadership. Some yearn for the good old days when we had it. Yet when we get it, we sometimes don't recognise it, and even if we do, we seldom reward it.

People always grumble about political leaders. But there is a deeper malaise afoot now. Zoom out from the daily inanity of the domestic news cycle. Zoom out even further from the point where you shake your head in disbelief at Trumpian political developments around the world or local Liberal Party madness. Consider something a little unlikely as a sign of our leadership discontents.

Young people's fiction these days comes in ever faster waves of franchises seeking to ride particular crazes: for wizards, zombies, vampires or the post-apocalyptic. In many of these books, TV series and films, the same themes recur: societies in which the rules have broken down, in which there are no people in positions of authority, or even formal leadership structures. These are stories built on disillusionment and a suspicion of social structure – which often acts as a threat to our heroes, who invariably are just average kids. Rugged individuals must make do, striving to stay alive, at least until the end of the book or episode.

Our young people absorb, but are also attracted to, these worlds with their broken-down societies or absent leaders. This might be no more than a reflection of the slightly maudlin phase many of us go through as teenagers. At first glance, an obsession with the post-apocalyptic would seem more understandable in those of us who grew up during the Cold War, rather than the second decade of the twenty-first century. But the disillusionment reflected in fictional domains coincides with the global return of the strongman to politics. And with these two conflicting trends comes a belated alarm that the world is not naturally tending to the Western democratic model that many of us smugly assumed had triumphed and become irresistible at the end of the Cold War.

*

In so many ways, the qualities and requirements of leadership are eternal. We have all read about the great figures of history, and that reading has shaped our views of what makes a true leader. But if I'm right about the changing expectations we have of politics – and if our institutions and institutional memory are being transformed – then there is much to say about how those human beings who have a will to influence others, and to power, rub up against the forces at play in modern politics.

This essay considers those forces, and how leaders and leadership are responding to them. It is just too easy to say our current leaders aren't up to scratch (even if they aren't). We need to have a more sophisticated discussion about what they might lack and how we judge what they need to give us. But instead, when our young people look back at the real world, they see a deep cynicism about political leaders but also an unhealthy obsession; and a focus not so much on what they might have achieved for their communities, but merely on their personal traits.

In Australia, for example, the recent debate about Adani's controversial proposed coalmine in central Queensland descended at one point into a discussion of Bill Shorten's personality and honesty, rather than the merits or risks of the massive project. It became a discussion of the different messages Shorten sent to different audiences and what this told us about his character.

Similarly, Malcolm Turnbull's prime ministership was overwhelmingly considered in light of his personal qualities and life story, with little regard given to the circumstances that constrained or shaped his day-to-day political management, let alone that the prime ministership is but one dynamic in a larger play of political forces. Turnbull's fractious and self-indulgent Coalition partners in the Nationals, the reckless wrecking of Tony Abbott: we just wanted the prime minister to make these things go away, or to govern as if they don't exist, just as we expected the same thing of Julia Gillard when it came to the realities of minority government.

Consider the Nationals. John Howard had leaders Tim Fischer and John Anderson to deal with. Tony Abbott, and in the early days Malcolm Turnbull, had Warren Truss. These men were sometimes idiosyncratic, sometimes dull, but ultimately committed to the Coalition and making it work.

Self-indulgence on a grand scale is a relatively recent thing in Australian federal politics. Of course, individuals have long blundered through the narrative from Canberra, causing chaos for the government or Opposition of the day, and providing colourful copy for journalists. From Jim Cairns and his "kind of love" for Junie Morosi, to Barnaby Joyce and his victimhood view of his imploding personal life, there has always been something colourful to watch in federal politics. But until the last ten years, politicians largely acted on the understanding that their individual actions ultimately had to take into account the good of the party and the survival of the government.

Not anymore.

The tearing down of Malcolm Turnbull's prime ministership has been perhaps the most incomprehensible example of this. Turnbull was destroyed by people in the Liberal Party who, whatever they said about trying to save the government, were actually prepared to lose it to achieve their ends.

Whether or not Barnaby Joyce was a more politically effective leader of the Nationals than some of his predecessors, the untrammelled licence with which he has approached his career – and the fact there were so few signs of commitment to making the Coalition with the Liberal Party, and therefore the government, function successfully – make him the embodiment of the new self-indulgence. He was committed to havoc from the time he entered federal parliament as a senator in 2005.

Labor has had its own waves of self-indulgence, notably in the vengeful form of Kevin Rudd. Though he was himself a victim of the factions, his downfall as prime minister followed a very short period of disloyalty, which stands in stark contrast to his own relentless undermining of his colleagues. Julia Gillard as prime minister had the smallest of circles of ministers on which to rely in government, with Rudd and his colleagues constantly circling.

Once Bob Brown left the Senate, the Greens – a bit like the latter-day Nationals – did not seem to have the pragmatic understanding that the end of Labor government would limit their capacity to influence policy.

It's not a question of feeling sorry for Turnbull or Gillard, but of understanding that a lack of internal discipline and room to manoeuvre circumscribes what leaders can do before they even get out of bed in the morning. Instead of such problems being recognised as impediments that have to be dealt with, they tend to be treated as not just the leader's own fault, but also a sign of weakness. Thus, even as the Nationals and the conservative rump of the Liberal Party provide the daily colour and debacle of today's episode of *The Young and the Restless*, the trend is still to focus on the leaders, rather than those around them. The discussion becomes a one- or two-man play under a single spotlight, instead of a chaotic musical where the whole stage is lit to reveal an all-star cast, an unruly chorus and a Wagnerian-sized orchestra. How likely is it that we will understand what is really driving events when we view them this way?

Until relatively recently, the idea of collective cabinet government set the frame for federal politics in Australia. Prime ministers may always have been first among equals, but the discussion was about how the prime minister wrangled the views of his colleagues, or led them to a particular view, as the first best exemplar of wider consensus-building. Alternatively, the narrative may have been about the tussle of a particular minister to sway his or her colleagues, or a battle among ministers for policy supremacy.

But now it is a leader who succeeds or fails alone.

Yet, in Australia at least, the evolving structures of our government – particularly the complexities of Federation – have reached a point where it is simply not possible for any one person to bring about a dramatic change in complex national policy (if it ever was), no matter how persuasive an advocate they might be, or how clever they show themselves to be at manipulating the system.

It's not that dramatic change isn't possible. It's not that we ultimately don't need someone to set a direction. It's just that any sort of transformation requires not only that a leader master the mechanics of two levels of government and the circumstances of the day, but also that the rest of us have a clear-eyed understanding of all the factors a leader must manipulate in order to bring about that change – so that we can decide whether we will follow, and what we really think of the person leading us.

Complex change, involving several levels of government and a multitude of political interests, requires more political time and space than we seem prepared to give our leaders these days.

Francis Fukuyama wrote recently:

> Liberal democracies invite popular participation and over time tend to proliferate rules that complicate decision-making. When such

> political systems combine with polarized or otherwise severely divided publics, the result is often political paralysis, which makes ordinary governing very difficult. India under the previous Congress Party government was a striking example of this, where infrastructure projects and needed economic reforms seemed beyond the government's ability to deliver. Something similar occurred in Japan and Italy, which often seemed paralysed in the face of long-term economic stagnation.
>
> One of the most prominent cases was the US, where an extensive set of constitutionally mandated checks and balances can be seen as a "vetocracy," i.e. the ability of small groups to veto action on the part of majorities. This is what has produced a yearly crisis in Congress over passing a budget, something that has not been accomplished under so-called "regular order" for at least a generation, and has blocked sensible reforms of health care, immigration, and financial regulation.
>
> This perceived weakness in the ability of democratic governments to make decisions and get things done is one of the things that set the stage for the rise of "would-be strongmen" who can break through the miasma of normal politics and achieve results. This was one of the reasons that India elected Narendra Modi, and why Shinzo Abe has become one of Japan's longest-serving prime ministers. Vladimir Putin's rise as a "strongman" came against the background of the chaotic Yeltsin years. And, finally, one of Donald Trump's selling points was that, as a successful businessman, he would be able to make the US government functional again.

In other words, it is not just we who are experiencing these symptoms of paralysis.

There was much of the appeal of the "would-be strongman" in the election of Tony Abbott in 2013. Having fomented an air of chaos, weakness and dysfunction around the man he deposed as Liberal leader, and then around the Rudd and Gillard governments, Abbott promised voters he would lead a government that would be "back in charge." Issues that had seemed to run out of control, not just of government but of voters, would be put back in their box: "boat people"; the "carbon tax" he argued the government wanted to introduce; national debt; expensive government projects; red tape.

Australia voted primarily for an end to the sense of chaos around the Labor government, but never quite embraced Abbott's strongman tactics in office, particularly when they were turned against voters themselves in the punitive 2014 Budget.

Turnbull's return to the Liberal leadership in 2015 could be seen as a rejection of the strongman, even if there was a yearning that he should shift politics back to some central place, from which it had been dislodged by Abbott.

Voters' frustration with Turnbull was not primarily over policy paralysis but because of a lack of any clear policy at all, or at least of the sort of policies many thought he would introduce. It was not complicated rules that thwarted Turnbull, nor a community-wide "vetocracy," but a "vetocracy" within his own parliamentary party. Turnbull's inability to wrangle these internal political forces – or perhaps his refusal to ostentatiously stare them down – left voters frustrated and ate away at his authority. The leadership challenge from Peter Dutton that emerged in August 2018 only highlighted all these trends: the self-indulgence, the lack of any commitment to collective responsibility; the complexity of policy issues; polarised and divided electorates; the slow undermining of prime ministerial authority. And, ominously, it pointed to the prospect of another tilt to the right, to populism and to strongman politics.

Finding a way to deal with these trends, something that eluded Malcolm Turnbull, was the real task facing Scott Morrison when he became prime minister in August 2018.

*

Internationally, Donald Trump seems to embody our very conflicting expectations and frustrations when it comes to leaders. We are as alarmed by the apparent powerlessness of American institutions to contain or direct him as we are by the erratic ignorance and nastiness of his actions. Yet a grudging respect sometimes sneaks into discussion of his actions. "Look," a political friend says one day in early 2018, when Trump has appeared to achieve a breakthrough on North Korea, but is also embroiled in a scandal about a payment to a porn star, "I abhor everything Trump stands for. He is an oaf. But you have to say this for him: when he is attacked, he doesn't back down, he doubles down." But leadership is, and should be seen as, more than simply a preparedness to "crash through or crash" or "not blink." It should be defined as a capacity to lead a community to accept change – even if that change is not a change for the better.

Paul Keating is often cited as an example of a true leader because of his "crash or crash through" style, yet the former prime minister would always say, "You have to bring the mob with you." He saw his job as setting the direction and then persuading enough people that he was right to enable him to follow that path.

Political leadership should be about building a consensus for change, giving people a map to follow, and bringing together different parties to achieve an outcome. Instead, discussion of leadership becomes about the machismo of individuals taking on the mob. There is something inherently undemocratic about this. It leads to a yearning for autocracy, and whether Americans realise or acknowledge it, they have given themselves someone who acts exactly like an autocrat whenever he is dealing with an issue on which he cannot be constrained by Congress.

The unresolved debate about leaders and the mob goes right back to Plato. But we don't seem to recognise that right now we are at one of those points in the never-ending debate where the struggle is particularly confused. The push and pull factors seem out of balance. Voters are disillusioned with people in positions of political leadership because they don't think they are being heard: disillusioned enough to become disengaged from politics or even to lose faith in democracy completely.

The result in democracies can vary. One outcome is a leader who relies almost solely on the good opinion of the people. That goodwill was once only tested at elections. Opinion polls have now made the test a continual one.

Another outcome is that leaders are marked down who are perceived to have failed to get past the institutions of democracy – Congress in the United States, the Senate here – to express the popular will; or alternatively, who win plaudits for bypassing or bludgeoning the system. Throughout his prime ministership, we saw Turnbull regularly criticised for not taking on his own party, or the parliament, on policy from climate change to same-sex marriage. Yet bludgeoning the democratic institutions is exactly, in extremis, what leaders whom we might not rate highly have done. We are right to criticise Turnbull for failing to persuade his party or the parliament on an issue. But is it right to criticise him for failing to bypass them? I don't think so.

The former Australian ambassador to the United States Kim Beazley correctly warned in mid-2016 – when not a lot of other people were doing so – that we should not complacently presume that Donald Trump would not win the Republican Party's presidential nomination, nor that he would not win the presidency. But Beazley's most interesting observation was that no one should presume that the congressional block that had bedevilled previous presidencies would necessarily stand in the way of Trump. That was because Congress could only stop presidents *doing* things. When presidents were trying to *undo* things, Congress was next to powerless.

As Opposition leader in Australia, Abbott gave the "undoing" stream of politics a good run. But in our system, it turned out that undoing things is often harder than it seems to be in the United States.

These observations lead us inevitably to a third outcome of the system being out of balance: voters seek leaders who seem strong and who advance black-and-white propositions and have the will to pursue them, even though that means not listening to what voters are saying. The normal order of things in a democracy would see a leader strike out on a particular policy path, advocate for it, and – they hope – win sufficient acceptance that enough of the people will follow them.

In normal times, there was also sometimes a clear-eyed recognition that people weren't following, or were rejecting where you were heading. One aspect of true leadership requires conceding that you were wrong to start with, or that circumstances have changed enough to make what was once a correct formula wrong. How often does that happen? Is that just because leaders won't admit that they were wrong? Or because they feel this would be political suicide? What tolerance do we have for leaders who admit that they were wrong? What space do we give them?

The shallowness of a discussion that simply equates leadership with the assertive personalities of our political leaders is only further confused by a failure to distinguish between leadership and political success. Political success implies popularity, whereas leadership often involves doing things that are not popular. Think about the expectation that underlies this trend of personality: the implication is that the fate of the nation rests entirely in the hands of one individual. That implies that if you change the national leader, you change the country – itself a twisting of the old adage that if you change the government, you change the country. The link between leadership and political success reveals itself most regularly in our obsession with opinion polls: yet a leader's rating is a measure of political *success*, not *leadership*. Edmund Burke famously said: "Your representative owes you, not his industry only, but his judgment; and he betrays instead of serving you if he sacrifices it to your opinion."

Leadership often involves widely unpopular decisions. Sure, if the leader can't eventually persuade people that the unpopular decisions are the right ones, he or she will suffer the electoral consequences. The eventual end of John Howard's prime ministership is generally linked to his pushing industrial relations reform with the wildly unpopular WorkChoices.

But he had also made other decisions that were unpopular, including to send more troops to Iraq in 2005. The Abbott/Hockey Budget of 2014 contained an array of unpopular decisions, which were presented as acts of tough leadership. But they were decisions that either explicitly broke election promises or which had not been foreshadowed. They involved a significant rewriting of people's understanding of the role of government: unemployment benefits would not be available to anyone until the age of twenty-five; a co-payment for visiting bulk-billing doctors shook the electorate's faith in the Coalition's support for Medicare; $80 billion was going to be slashed from health and education through cuts to the states. These are examples of decisions that might have involved the leadership quality of bravery, but not necessarily good political judgment, and certainly not the skills to bring people with you. They are not decisions that you would put in the category of great political success.

Bob Hawke and Paul Keating were able to push through a range of unpopular economic decisions, from removing tariffs that protected industry to restraining wages in a centralised arbitration system, despite resistance from some in their own party and from those who were affected by the decisions. They could do this because, in the first round of the debate, they found voices in support of the decisions within business and the media and, in the second round, they persuaded enough voters that the moves were in the long-term interest of the country, even if they came at a short-term cost.

Equally, a leader might enjoy great poll ratings – on the back of leadership cowardice in the form of policies that seek no greater outcome than to lock in the support of voters. This is where we enter the territory of populism.

There is also a swathe of policies, both good and bad, for which leaders often prefer not to take any "leadership" credit. Immigration is the classic, persistent example in Australia. Immigration has never stopped since white settlement and only escalated after World War II. But it is not and has never been popular policy. Few political leaders today are prepared to champion the record-high levels of immigration of the past couple of decades, instead emphasising that these are driven heavily by markets and highlighting the areas where they themselves have stopped or slowed immigration. Other politicians have emerged to criticise immigration.

In January 2015, Turnbull, as communications minister, talked about policy leadership in a speech at the US–Australia dialogue.

> Many would add it means taking unpopular decisions. I would rephrase that by saying it means taking decisions which may not be popular but will be accepted because the public understands why they have to be taken.
>
> Leaders must be decision-makers, but they must also be, above all, explainers and advocates, unravelling complex issues in clear language that explains why things have to change and why the government cannot solve every problem.

Later that same year, he gave two reasons why he should replace Tony Abbott as Liberal leader and prime minister. The first was that Abbott didn't have, and wasn't selling, a coherent strategy, particularly on economic matters. The second was that opinion polls relentlessly showed that Abbott had lost voters' confidence. It says much that the second point is raised much more than the first in assessments of Turnbull's time as prime minister.

The shortcomings of linking leadership and political success are ultimately exposed by the evidence that even four prime ministers in five years hasn't wildly changed the nature of our country – except perhaps to make us feel less settled about its outlook. We find ourselves in a position where we look with horror at the rise of the strongman in other countries, yet were unhappy with a prime minister who would not take a stand at home.

We judge political leaders by their popularity rather than their ideas. And we seem to have little tolerance for the details of new policy – wherever they come from.

In Australia, while we have increasingly been focusing our political debates through the prism of our leaders' personalities, the landscape in which their soap operas are played out has been changing. The ideological structure of our political parties – as in many other Western democracies – reflects the capital/labour divide that dominated political debate for much of the twentieth century. Yet what was once a clear divide has become very blurry in recent decades. That has had implications for the influence and organisation of our major political parties. Their grassroots membership is in decline. More importantly, their capacity to organise around and campaign on an idea is in decline. Without a central idea to frame their cause, the parties have lost not only their clarity of message but also their commitment to a higher goal. Individual MPs no longer have a sense that they are working towards a greater, common good. A parliamentary party room can be much more easily pulled apart because of this lack of central purpose.

The stark result is that leaders of political parties begin their time in the job with a much shakier and more transient hold on power than leaders of even twenty years ago. That is, they have less authority and less freedom to move. This is the case even though our political leaders have increasingly become the only players on the stage. Our world used to be populated by a menagerie of figures who offered leadership. They represented institutions that once played powerful roles in both our political and community discussions, but which are now in decline or collapse.

Perhaps this is another reason why divisions in a parliamentary party room seem so much more important than they once did: few centres of leadership in the community are seen to have the same level of influence as politicians do. Debates which might have once taken place publicly among politicians, church leaders and scientists, for example, are now fought out by proxies in the party room – by politicians, who are the only ones with sufficient status to argue. All others are "mere" stakeholders.

For a while, defining people as "stakeholders" seemed to acknowledge that they had a legitimate voice or role in debate. But the term has increasingly been used in a more derogatory sense: that is, "stakeholder" is used interchangeably with "vested interest" to suggest that the party involved is speaking only from the point of view of narrow self-interest. Now, this may often be the case. (Politics is supposed to be how we find outcomes that satisfy narrow interests while also achieving an outcome in the broad interest.) But by lumping together all those who appeal to politicians as stakeholders, it implies both that they come to the table compromised, and that it is only politicians who can somehow rise above this to see the greater good.

Over the centuries, there has perhaps been no more powerful group of leaders – or institution – than religious elders. In the Western world, the Christian churches – and their leaders – survived the collapse of monarchies and revolutions. Christianity provided the backdrop against which systems of government were tested. The churches' influence and assertion of power put armies into the field, and helped provide the constraint against which those trying to define new post-revolutionary power structures had to push. They could muster earthly power as well as claim a heavenly mandate to assert a moral, as well as political, authority.

The churches have given countless generations a framework by which to live and against which to judge themselves. Yet the influence of Christian churches in Australia is now marginal at best. The shocking details of child abuse may currently be stripping the churches of the last vestiges of their authority as the arbiters of moral behaviour, but the capacity of the churches to sway an argument in the Australian political realm has been in decline for decades. And it is not only the priests and ministers of the European-based churches who do not have the sway over their congregations they once did. We are also suspicious of, even hostile to, the influence of leaders of religions newer to our shores, such as Islam.

Some of the harder-line conservative Christian groups have been resorting of late to attempts to gain control of the conservative political parties. But that is very different from having open and public influence on our national debates. And it remains to be seen whether the strategy will be successful, or simply lead to even greater marginalisation of the parties they would use to build their influence.

Of course, there has been no greater battle for organised religion over the centuries than the one with science. But our scientific leaders have not gained greater prominence with the decline of religious leaders. Most spectacularly, the collapse a decade ago of the perceived credibility of the case for escalating anthropogenic climate change was a dazzling and terrifying political demolition of an idea in the English-speaking world. It was a nail in the coffin of any deference to science and orderly thinking. Scientists get very little kudos these days. The idea that science, as a rational form of thinking, might be something of value seems diminished.

Nor does any side seem to have emerged victorious in the battle of ideas or ideologies, particularly the battle between labour and capital which dominated the twentieth century. Socialism as the utopia of the workers failed. But as with the battle between religion and science, any expectation that the collapse of socialism might reinforce the victory of capitalism has gone unfulfilled. Capitalism seems to be in almost as much trouble as socialism. The institutions that fought out these battles in Australia are suffering as sharp a downgrade in the community's mind as the ideas they championed. The trade unions are in decline. Individual business leaders have little sway, even if they may, in recent decades, have won the battle over the freeing-up of markets.

Much of the current political debate about growing inequality, both in Australia and globally, is a rejection of the "trickle-down," free-market or neoliberal economics that has dominated policy-making and politics in the West. But a side effect of this has been the discrediting and marginalisation of economics and economists in the public debate. We may think the world is still too enamoured of the free market. Economists are not always right. But for the past decade, while politicians have continued to use the language of economics, we have been in something of a twilight world, where economists don't shape the terms of the discussion but there is no clear – dare one say "evidence-based"? – method of thinking to replace the love affair with free-market economics.

Economists, who once loomed over our politics, have retreated into their corners in the wake of the global financial crisis and growing inequality. A most spectacular example of this occurred during the Brexit debate in 2016. The United Kingdom's then justice secretary, Michael Gove, was campaigning for Britain to leave the European Union. Gove was not one of those raging against immigration, but rather arguing more calmly for greater self-reliance. But when asked to name a single economist who thought Brexit was a good idea, Gove (now rather infamously) refused, saying that, "People in this country have had enough of experts." A number of economists had actually been arguing in favour of Britain's exit from the EU. The point, though, was that Gove opted not to name them, and, as *The Financial Times* reported, preferred "to focus on how economists and economic organisations had failed to predict the financial crisis." "I'm not asking the public to trust me. I'm asking them to trust themselves," he said.

Educators – be they schoolteachers or university lecturers – do not have the standing they once did. Teachers are dismissed and discounted because they work for either the public or private system, or by derisory typecasting as advocates of one teaching philosophy or another. Lecturers can be similarly typecast, but often carry the extra baggage of constraint on participation in public discourse imposed as a condition of their funding. Like doctors or judges, they find that their underlying authority is not necessarily at issue, but the legitimacy of their contribution to the political debate is under constant challenge.

Even in the cultural realm, we too often deride the figures to whom we would once have listened. So often it is artists who lead the way in changes in thinking, or who capture a moment. Yet artists are lumped together, labelled as "leftists" and dismissed.

All this only puts more weight, or expectation, on political leadership. Our political leaders are not just asked to advocate an idea about where the country is headed. They are asked to move into the moral realm in the absence of churches, asked to define what is acceptable behaviour in business, asked to define the nature of our culture and national values. They may have done this in the past, but the point is that they were once only one set of voices in a national conversation. Now their interventions are the overwhelming ones in an era when other participants' roles have been diminished.

Think of how politicians' voices – and the reporting of their manoeuvrings – dominated the debate on same-sex marriage. Yes, there were voices from the community, but there was a feeling that they carried little weight compared to the varying views of politicians. That might make sense at the pointy end of a legislative discussion. But it seemed the community pressure and debate that eventually led to the parliamentary discussion was never quite taken seriously, simply because politicians were refusing to take it seriously. Yet that same-sex marriage prevailed was ultimately an outcome of unrelenting pressure from outside the system, and, when it came to the plebiscite, of crucial community validation that forced the paralysed political leadership to move at last.

Perhaps there is no more spectacular example of this trend than the closing down or ignoring of Indigenous contributions to the debate about Indigenous affairs. Having committed to some form of recognition of Indigenous Australians in the constitution, politicians started an extensive process of consultation and deliberation by panels of experts. But when Indigenous groups who had status in that process came up with a very different proposal, it was dismissed by the government.

Politicians dominate our discussions on a day-to-day basis, but the demise of other frameworks to support the clash of ideas and institutions leaves a void too easily filled by leadership based on emotion and prejudice. History tells us that this can lead to jingoism and scapegoating. When the status of other institutions has been diminished, the risk of political leaders emerging to exploit our baser instincts is dramatically increased. One of the few structures to survive the decline in institutional leadership and not be subsumed by political leaders has been the military. Sure, governments might take on the language and mantle of national security and defence. But this also seems to be the one remaining area where they defer to the experts. Is it any wonder, therefore, that our defence and national security debates become the hunting ground of politicians seeking to make their reputations?

*

While these changes to institutional authority have been occurring, another type of change has also affected the capacity to lead.

Information has always been a hot currency of power. Access to more and better information has given governments and other powerful institutions the upper hand in debate. Think of the way the government of the day has been able to assert its executive right to take Australian troops into war based on undisclosed intelligence. That advantage used to be even greater because of delays in publicly available information making its way from the other side of the world. We relied on governments to tell us what was happening. But that advantage has been whittled away by online communication.

In a similar way, the fact most voters had no ready access to advice available to the government – even when it wasn't confidential – meant it was much easier for governments to set the terms of a debate, and much more necessary for the rest of us to take them at their word. An expert report on the future of the energy system, for example, would only be read by the handful of people involved in the debate, and its executive summary by journalists. Now such a report is available online for anyone with an interest in seeing it.

The irony is that while the government might have lost its upper hand and the information available to voters is actually greater, this has not made debate more informed. The brutal reality seems to be that no more people read a lot of this material. Instead, we are swamped by the sheer magnitude of what we could read if we just had the time.

Significantly, the media have responded to the change by working on the presumption that, since the report in question is readily available, their role is to "add value" by pushing the story forward rather than lingering on the substance of the report. The story, even on the day new information emerges, becomes the political response to it.

This change in the information balance affects not just politicians, but leaders in other fields. Patricia Seemann founded the 3am Group of business leaders some years ago to reflect on the compounding difficulties faced by chief executives in an information-rich, globalised world. She observed that technological change meant that these days:

> You cannot know any more as a leader. Therefore, your role as a leader has changed to becoming the one figuring out what the best way is to frame problems, what the most important questions are to be asked.

In politics, this translates, at its worst, as spin. More benignly, it keeps the focus on the questions that have been asked, rather than the answers.

Access to information has also changed in another way. We once formed opinions from the same sources. As Barack Obama told the writer Marilynne Robinson in 2015:

> Part of the challenge is – and I see this in our politics – is a common conversation. It's not so much, I think, that people don't read at all; it's that everybody is reading [in] their niche, and so often, at least in the media, they're reading stuff that reinforces their existing point of view ... other than the Super Bowl, we don't have a lot of common reference points. And you can argue that that's part of the reason why our politics has gotten so polarized, is that – when I was growing up, if the president spoke to the country, there were three stations and every city had its own newspaper and they were going to cover that story. And that would last for a couple of weeks, people talking about what the president had talked about.

> Today, my poor press team, they're tweeting every two minutes because some new thing has happened, which then puts a premium on the sensational and the most outrageous or a conflict as a way of getting attention and breaking through the noise – which then creates, I believe, a pessimism about the country because all those quiet, sturdy voices that we were talking about at the beginning, they're not heard.

What once were considered policy issues for the experts tend to become political issues. Issues that would have been fought out more equally by leaders of different sectors of the community, who were regarded as representatives with standing and something to contribute, become matters for contention on a crowded political battlefield.

This much-changed landscape has implications for the capacity of leaders to lead. It has implications for the sorts of leaders who are thrown up by the political process. Consider the last few leadership changes in federal politics. Malcolm Turnbull was made leader not because the Liberal Party believed in, or agreed with, the philosophical positions he was believed to hold, but because they thought he could garner more votes than Tony Abbott. Kevin Rudd was made leader twice, and deposed once, by the Labor Party for the same reason. Scott Morrison was made leader for no more positive reason than that he was not Peter Dutton. We talk a lot about the mechanics of a coup: which factions are supporting which contender. But the endgame is much more straightforward: leaders are elected who are expected to be "popular," even if they do not represent the views of their own party. Little wonder that voters seem so regularly confused about what our leaders stand for. These leaders find themselves on much less secure, much narrower platforms, denied the support of clear frameworks of ideas, yet they are expected to have an opinion on everything.

As I've argued, the standing of other institutions and leaders has been degraded. But political leaders also have less authority and speak with less clarity in this environment as they endlessly seek to avoid offending anyone. Voter disillusionment lies in empty phrases, yet, in the contrary way of politics, the political response to not having much to say, and not many people to say it to, is to perpetually campaign. As soon as the parliament rises, the prime minister and Opposition leader scurry off to another marginal electorate. When the parliament sits, they use it as a backdrop for political attacks on their opponents.

The impact of perpetual campaigning has changed the day-to-day workload and focus of our leaders. It inevitably means the conversation is about political success. The value of governing inevitably diminishes. And it makes them very time-poor, in a world of increasingly complex problems and increasingly impatient demands for answers to those problems.

We don't like to be told that issues are sometimes irresolvable, and we dislike political conflict. Obama observed after he left office that:

> One of the interesting things about the presidency – and again I don't think this is unique to the US Presidency, I think it's true for leaders of large organisations – but obviously the consequences for the US President could be higher. You notice very quickly that nothing reaches your desk that is entirely solved. I mean, by definition if somebody could solve it, then they would have and you'd never see it. So the only thing that lands on your desk are things that nobody else could figure out and inevitably will leave somebody angry and dissatisfied when the decision is made.

This leads to a final shift. While so much of the modern political narrative focuses on leadership dramas, the striking thing about the past decade has been how the broader political discussion has shifted, with the blurring and breakdown of clear ideological divides, to the personal qualities of political followers. Whether we are trying to recognise our own country in its relationship with leaders from Kevin Rudd to Pauline Hanson, or to understand people who voted for Donald Trump, or staring longingly at what we see in leaders like Angela Merkel, but being disconcerted by the voters who put the anti-immigration Alternative for Germany into the Bundestag, we increasingly talk about the electorate as much as the leaders. There is a kind of volatile electoral identity politics in play, of manipulation and reaction.

Our politicians' speeches seek to channel voters rather than argue a case for where they want to lead them.

Despite the professionalisation of politics and the vast quantities of money spent on research, politicians seem to know less about the people who follow them – or don't – than ever before.

Class-based agendas, and even ideological agendas, have become hopelessly mixed up.

What does a leader rest his or her leadership on in that case? Are leaders around the world all responding in the same way to these new challenges? And how do they seek to control the last remaining variables in their decision-making – the time and space to think, advocate and act?

In February 2018, in a boardroom high above Melbourne, a group has gathered to judge the first McKinnon Prize, established to encourage and promote political leadership in Australia. Two former prime ministers, John Howard and Julia Gillard, sit on the judging panel. The criteria for judging the prize says much about what we yearn for in our leaders. It seeks to recognise, at all levels of government, those "who have successfully tackled vital issues of public policy, overcome adversity and achieved real change for the public good." After a long day of deliberations, the prize for political leader of the year is awarded to Dean Smith, the Western Australian Liberal senator at the heart of the push for same-sex marriage legislation. Vonda Malone is awarded the prize for emerging political leader, for her work as mayor of the Torres Shire Council.

During the day, all the factors that determine a leader's success, and the handicaps they might have carried, were considered. Often, it was a matter of trying to determine just how difficult a working environment leaders faced in achieving their goals. What hostility did they encounter? What support did they garner from their colleagues? What was the exact nature of their role in a debate? Was success necessary in measuring political leadership, or was just trying something but being defeated good enough? The conversation ebbed and flowed, but by the end of it the panel awarded the prize to Smith because of the courage he had shown campaigning on an issue that was divisive within his own party, and for his success in steering the required legislative changes through a parliamentary committee.

The McKinnon Prize strives to capture and encourage what political leadership can be. But it doesn't quite capture what we want our political leaders to be, which is something different. A foreign diplomat marvelled to me recently at the obsession with leadership in Australia: not just political leadership, but the number of seminars and conferences and courses that are regularly advertised for business executives, and the number of articles written about corporate leadership.

It is worth stepping out of the Australian realm for a time to consider what leadership is, and what defines and confines it. It is also worth remembering that political leadership does not necessarily result in happy ends. Shakespeare wrote in *Richard II*:

> Let us sit upon the ground
> And tell sad stories of the death of kings;
> How some have been deposed; some slain in war,
> Some haunted by the ghosts they have deposed;
> Some poison'd by their wives: some sleeping kill'd;
> All murder'd: for within the hollow crown
> That rounds the mortal temples of a king
> Keeps Death his court and there the antic sits,
> Scoffing his state and grinning at his pomp,
> Allowing him a breath, a little scene,
> To monarchise, be fear'd and kill with looks,
> Infusing him with self and vain conceit,
> As if this flesh which walls about our life,
> Were brass impregnable, and humour'd thus
> Comes at the last and with a little pin
> Bores through his castle wall, and farewell king!

Here are the delusions of immortality of so many leaders, and the reality of their fragile reign, even if these days their demise does not often involve being slain, poisoned or murdered. Nevertheless, much of our political narrative still comprises gaudy attempts to mimic Shakespeare's dramas, rather than chronicles of events or decisions which affect the rest of us. That is, it is all about the players on stage, not the impact of their actions outside the theatre.

The intensely personal focus on leaders once made a lot more sense. Historian John Lewis Gaddis reflected on the leadership styles of two of history's great rivals, Elizabeth I and Philip II of Spain, in his book *On Grand Strategy*, noting that "the health, mental stability, and reproductive prowess of princes could cause faiths to rise and nations to fall." These were leaders from the long centuries when hereditary leadership and Divine Right, or at least the occasional heavenly intervention, were not questioned. The very future of a nation was bound up in the person of its leader.

Equally, history is so often portioned off by name: Caesar, Henry VIII, Napoleon, Hitler, Mao and Stalin. These names notably belong to autocrats or despots who dominated the societies in which they ruled. We are fascinated by their rise to power, and their use of it. Writing in *Young Hitler*, the Australian historian Paul Ham observed that:

> Germany's newly minted leader did not step out of a gaseous haze to rule the world. The Führer emerged incrementally ... from a series of bumbling failures, stunning successes and the application of political skills he had not yet realized he possessed.

Along the way, he was prepared to draw close to the most unlikely allies:

> That Hitler briefly cosied up to revolutionary communists in 1919 should not baffle us. We demand linear correctness in the lives of politicians and leaders even as we ourselves act in inconsistent and contrarian ways.

We struggle to imagine how a figure like Adolf Hitler could possibly have emerged in a civilised country like Germany. It seems even more unimaginable that we would in our own country tolerate any such figure who threatened our institutions and, ultimately, the democratic balance in favour of a more autocratic system, even without the particular horrors associated with Hitler. Ham's point is that history is rarely a straight line; instead, we become accustomed to gradual shifts in tolerance and in the balances of power.

Once autocrats get to the top, whether through divine right, coup or a less obvious assault on democracy, they invest considerable time, money and energy in linking their identity and authority with that of the state.

But being powerful is not necessarily the same as leading. And leading in a parliamentary democracy like ours creates a very different set of dynamics between the leaders and the led. As we have seen, our governments run on the principle of collective responsibility rather than chief executive leadership, and governments must keep going back to voters to be granted the authority to keep leading us. That should mean that we judge leaders in this context: that we balance the responsibility and qualities of our prime ministers (at the federal level) against their colleagues' performance and qualities. But we don't.

We rarely talk these days about "the government" or "the Opposition." But we do talk a lot about the battle between "the prime minister" and "the leader of the Opposition." It was not always thus. There has obviously always been a focus on leaders, but, as I recall it, the way earlier governments were reported involved a much greater sense of the dynamics within a government, a sense that governments – and Oppositions – formed a complex personality of their own beyond that of the leader. Similarly, battles between ministers, or factions, or ideas, within a government or an Opposition were not seen merely through the prism of challenges to the leadership or authority of the prime minister.

Before the Whitlam government became framed in many people's minds by the nature of its demise, its internal dynamics gave rise to stories of battles between Whitlam, Cairns and Connor. We all knew who Lionel Murphy, Bill Hayden and Lance Barnard were. Ministers had their own agendas to push and on which to persuade their colleagues and the rest of us. This was the case even with a larger-than-life prime minister, who had his own very clear "vision" for Australia.

Similarly, the Fraser government was not just a story about Malcolm Fraser, but about the battles inside his cabinet, the influence of the Country Party cabal around him, the increasing tensions over policy between Fraser and his treasurer, John Howard.

The *Labor in Power* series put on our televisions some of the epic internal policy battles of the Hawke and Keating years, from the consumption tax to the Coronation Hill uranium mine. Policy battles were still a feature of the way we saw the Howard government. But maybe it was Howard's ultimate political dominance over his government – the perception that he alone was the master tactician and author of its fate – that helped shift the way governments were reported towards an obsessive focus on the leader.

Kevin Rudd certainly demanded a level of obeisance from his ministers. And there had been a creeping tide of control by the prime minister's office since the Howard era that put the leader front and centre. The net result is that, when combined with our tendency to adopt the American style of reporting on a presidential system, the levers of power within a government, let alone the wider political structure, are downplayed or dismissed. Their legitimacy is questioned. The right of the parliament – and particularly the Senate – to challenge the executive government is regarded with outrage. This inevitably leads to an obsession with personal authority and charisma, and exacerbates the trend which sees reporters at polling booths on election day asking voters: did you vote for Scott Morrison or Bill Shorten?

But holding the position of leader is a very different thing from providing leadership. If we set aside our obsession with the figure of the leader, what does leadership itself consist of? There is still considerable confusion about this. Often it is associated with machismo or doggedness. Almost always it is seen through the lens of formal positions of leadership or authority.

In 1994, Ronald Heifetz, from the Kennedy School of Government at Harvard University, wrote a book called *Leadership Without Easy Answers*, in which he argues that leadership, power and formal authority too often get confused and need to be carefully distinguished. He defines leadership as helping a community embrace change. That is, a leader is the facilitator of a group that has to confront an issue, though just how that facilitation works is a complex matter. Heifetz is not suggesting that leadership is merely a matter of leading a group discussion. Instead, he offers fascinating case studies, from Lyndon Johnson to George H.W. Bush, from Hitler to Gandhi. The change a group has to confront may not be a happy one – and if you wonder why Hitler is included, it is because Heifetz argues that leaders can often lead a group to a catastrophic response when confronting an issue. Wherever the group is headed, though, leadership is about offering a map through an issue, giving people a clear option to deal with a problem. It might involve corralling various factions to a compromise. Significantly, Heifetz argues that political leadership is not necessarily about having a vision and pursuing it, but about a range of other skills with which to "read" and push a community.

Lyndon Johnson's leadership is perhaps the most compelling example Heifetz gives to illustrate this point. He analyses how Johnson's political skills – which included his great understanding of the politics of the American South – allowed him to oversee major breakthroughs on civil rights, including the 1964 *Civil Rights Act* and the 1965 *Voting Rights Act*, by both assisting and enlisting black leaders, such as Martin Luther King, to achieve change. The *Civil Rights Act* gave Washington the right to end segregation in the South. It was quickly followed by the *Voting Rights Act*, which outlawed the practice of using literacy tests – which often had trick questions, not unlike those once used to enforce the White Australia policy – and poll taxes as a way of assessing whether anyone was fit or unfit to vote. Unlike John F. Kennedy, who was lionised for his inspirational speeches, Johnson's skills lay in the mastery of knowing when to act and when not to. Heifetz writes that Johnson "intended to mobilize the nation as a whole to work on issues that had been avoided for nearly two hundred years."

> Yet mobilizing the society to tackle hard problems and learn new ways require far more than fashioning deals in the legislature; it required public leadership. Johnson had to identify the adaptive challenges facing the nation, regulate the level of distress, counteract work-avoiding distractions, place responsibility where it belonged and protect voices of leadership in the community.

He documents how President Johnson responded to, and used, protests in Selma, Alabama, in 1965 to advance his cause. Black civil rights protesters, including Martin Luther King, attempted to march from Selma to the state capital of Montgomery to register black voters, but were met with deadly violence from local authorities and white vigilantes. Johnson intervened through a nationally televised address on 15 March 1965 to pledge his support for the protesters and promote the voting rights bill. Six days later, 2000 people set out for Montgomery, protected by US Army troops and Alabama National Guard forces that Johnson had placed under federal control, reaching the state capital four days later.

For Heifetz, Johnson's negotiations during those crucial days in 1965 showed mastery by knowing how far things could be pushed at a particular time, and where the barriers were. He also constructed situations that gave his opponents cover or ways out of positions that had become untenable for them and everyone else. Heifetz argues:

> We often think that leadership means having a clear vision and the capacity to persuade people to make it real. In this case, Johnson had authored no vision.
>
> Johnson's leadership lay in his wherewithal to give meaning to the crisis and avoid the common pitfall of restoring order prematurely. He let the heat remain high. He kept people's attention on the issues generating the heat. He shifted responsibility to those with the problem. He let the dissident voices be heard … and he seized the moment to turn the nation's emerging values into potent legislation.

In stark contrast, Johnson's policy on Vietnam was a disaster because he "took the stance that leaders lead and followers follow":

> In formulating foreign policy, Johnson seems to have ignored the lessons of his domestic policy successes … in setting and implementing Vietnam policy, Johnson made fatal mistakes by acting the part of the lone warrior and by creeping up in stealth not only on his enemy but also on his own constituents … he failed to face the

> nation with the adaptive challenge of Vietnam, to keep the level of distress within a productive range, to discipline attention, to distribute responsibility, and to use dissent as a source of insight and options.

Heifetz's way of looking at the world can short-circuit the big academic theories about what makes leaders great – theories, for example, which argue that leaders emerge from specific circumstances, or have a special capacity to see through the smoke of battle to the real target of their attack.

It also allows a study of leaders who emerge despite not holding formal positions of authority and power – that is, it broadens our sense of leadership. Gandhi's power and influence, for example, came from leading campaigns of civil disobedience outside political structures in South Africa and India, long before he became associated with the Indian National Congress.

In contemporary Australia, the group who pushed for changes to same-sex marriage are a classic case of leadership from outside positions of formal authority. Heifetz makes the point that women are, time and again, the prime examples of leadership without authority.

> Leadership may more often emerge from the foot of the table, but that is not where we spend most of our time looking ... That I use the metaphor of the table, with the head traditionally a man and the foot characteristically a woman, is no accident. Leadership without authority has been the domain to which women have been restricted for ages. Having been denied formal authority roles in most societies, some women have learned ... not to try leading at all.

I asked Julia Gillard about this earlier this year and she warmed to the theme, arguing that all of us, not just men, have to change our perceptions of what authority looks like, because for most of us it looks like a bloke in a suit. She spoke of how women have to surmount even this first step to leadership when denied the initial authority of being seen as potential leaders in a room, rather than service staff. We pondered the difference in the way Hillary Clinton was treated by the media and her political opponents when she was a senator from New York, and secretary of state, and when she was front and centre as a presidential candidate. Clinton seemed a less threatening figure when she was in the former roles: rather than the central figure of authority, she was someone working within a system.

*

This essay has been written against the backdrop of extraordinary and troubling developments in global leadership. We have seen Xi Jinping rise to a position of dominance in China, confirmed by changes that effectively make him leader for life. In Russia, Vladimir Putin continues to entrench himself and exert influence beyond his country's borders. In Turkey, Recep Tayyip Erdoğan has extended his executive powers and curbed political and press freedom. But it is in the most powerful nation on earth, which we may think we understand better than those other countries, and which seems to be more like our own, that Donald Trump almost singlehandedly has been twisting and warping the exercise of leadership, authority and power.

At home, he practises the politics of the strongman and thumbs his nose – if not raises his middle finger – at institutional elites. Around the globe, he has been withdrawing America as global leader of the world order. Yet he has also been asserting his role on the world stage by confronting North Korea and Iran, with as yet unknown consequences. Trump has used the authority of presidential office with a casual disregard, which at times can only be seen as based on a complete incomprehension of what he is doing, to pursue vendettas against those by whom he feels personally affronted or challenged. He has authority and power but, on the Heifetz definition, fails many of the leadership tests. He has mobilised his community, or "base," but offered them simple solutions rather than challenged them to tackle thorny problems. His supporters do not have to make difficult decisions. It is Trump's many scapegoats who bear the brunt of those decisions.

Rather than regulate and control the shape of the public discourse, Trump lets it career out of control, and provides distractions via Twitter. He does not corral dissidents but tries to destroy their credibility. And in his world, dissidents are anyone who dares to call out statements that are untrue. Trump's mastery is not of propaganda but of destruction of the credibility of information.

Yet he has been elected by voters yearning for someone who can make them feel powerful, and who feel the pull of a strongman, a pull that can be just as strong as the one felt by those who yearn for a leader with a vision, as those who voted for Barack Obama in 2008 did.

A system that imbues one individual with such status is always going to throw up huge expectations of what that person can do. Writing in *The New Yorker* in October 2014, a former speechwriter for Bill Clinton, Jeff Shesol, reflected on the expectations that surrounded Obama:

> that moment in most presidencies when a good number of Americans are able to convince themselves that we might be in the presence of a great man, and that his greatness will be manifest. That this is the man who has the answers. When it becomes clear that he doesn't, we never quite forgive him for it.

Earlier in 2014, Obama had talked about "that business about the great-man theory of history." "The President of the United States cannot remake our society, and that's probably a good thing," he said. On reflection, he added: "Not 'probably.' It's definitely a good thing."

Shesol noted that, "despite the grand hopes and hype of the 2008 campaign, this tempering of ambitions, this recognition – and acceptance – of the constraints on Presidential power has been a leitmotif of the Obama Presidency." Over the years, "Obama and his advisors have issued a long string of statements to this effect: on foreign policy, 'leading from behind'; on the limits of executive authority, 'there's no shortcut to democracy'; on civil rights, we must sometimes take 'a quarter of a loaf or half a loaf.' Shesol quotes author Aaron David Miller, in his book *The End of Greatness*, declaring it time for America to "get over the greatness thing" and "come to terms with the limits of a president's capacity to fix things."

Obama himself reflected on what leaders could achieve when he delivered the Nelson Mandela Annual Lecture in Johannesburg in July 2018. He argued that "the progressive, democratic vision that Nelson Mandela represented in many ways set the terms of international political debate." However, that did not mean "that vision was always victorious, but it set the terms, the parameters; it guided how we thought about the meaning of progress, and it continued to propel the world forward." Implicit in the speech, once more, was a rejection of the idea that one person can change the world, even as he outlined his argument that Mandela had shown that one man could set the terms of the discussion.

Obama argued that dealing with an increasingly dangerous world requires a recognition that there are many forces at work creating those dangers, and a sense of collective spirit. The global financial crisis had dealt a near mortal blow to the credibility of the international system and to "the faith in experts in places like Washington or Brussels." The result was that the "politics of fear and resentment and retrenchment" began to appear.

"Strongman politics are ascendant suddenly, whereby elections and some pretence of democracy are maintained – the form of it – but those in power seek to undermine every institution or norm that gives democracy meaning," the former president said, in comments taken to be a rare shot at his successor. "Right now," he said, "we don't just need one leader, we don't just need one inspiration – what we badly need right now is that collective spirit."

So here is the modern leadership dilemma in an Obama–Trump nutshell. On the one hand, there is Barack Obama, who is seen in most brutal terms as a choker by some of those closest to him. As David Runciman wrote in *The London Review of Books*, he is a man of contradictions: "the dreamer and the realist, the man who thinks anything is still possible and the man who has done his best, then shrugs his shoulders and walks away." In office Obama choked, we are told, because he acknowledged the need to build a consensus on change and had the oratorical power to persuade, but never seemed convinced that he should, or indeed could, force an issue. He gets a lot done at home. There is a big reform agenda he can point to. But you wonder whether the wily senator from the South, Lyndon Johnson, would have sensed a moment on, say, gun control and been able to translate the moment of one of those horrendous school shootings into some form of change.

Obama framed debates on issues. He worked the system and maintained the pressure to get healthcare reforms through Congress. But on the international stage, his legacy is seen as one of blinking on the big strategic calls in the Middle East and the Ukraine. (Foreign policy, as I shall discuss later, is an entirely different area of leadership.)

Leadership, as I said at the beginning of this essay, is a two-way thing. The question I ponder is whether the rest of us are prepared to give leaders like Obama the space to find a compromise, or the support to push through a deal.

On the other hand, there is Donald Trump.

Americans certainly didn't get over the greatness thing, as Aaron David Miller urged them to do in 2014. Not only did they elect a president who promised to "Make America Great Again," they elected a president who promised to ride roughshod over the political system, and proceeded to do so. Whatever else has happened in the presidency of Donald Trump, he has restored a sense of authority to the presidency, though not necessarily in a good way.

In the great Heifetz troika, Trump has authority and he has power. But does that make him a leader? Despite his erratic and half-arsed intervention in North Korea, his overarching direction in international politics has been active withdrawal by the United States from global leadership. At home, Trump is too impatient to lead the American public anywhere. He might be able to rouse sentiment, but that is not necessarily enough.

He has posed an "adaptive challenge" – of persuading America that it can become great by pursuing a set of policies that are the direct opposites of what made it great. But he has no interest in managing the distress level, even less in attention to discipline, or in focusing attention. He only wants to distribute responsibility to a collection of scapegoats.

Is Donald Trump a kind of throwback, a new incarnation of an old type? In another article in *The New Yorker*, this time in 2018, Miranda Carter reflected on the similarities between Trump and Kaiser Wilhelm II. In "What Happens When a Bad-Tempered, Distractible Doofus Runs an Empire?" Carter wrote:

> One of the many things that Wilhelm was convinced he was brilliant at, despite all evidence to the contrary, was "personal diplomacy," fixing foreign policy through one-on-one meetings with other European monarchs and statesmen. In fact, Wilhelm could do neither the personal nor the diplomacy, and these meetings rarely went well. The Kaiser viewed other people in instrumental terms, was a compulsive liar, and seemed to have a limited understanding of cause and effect. In 1890, he let lapse a long-standing defensive agreement with Russia – the German Empire's vast and sometimes threatening eastern neighbour. He judged, wrongly, that Russia was so desperate for German good will that he could keep it dangling. Instead, Russia immediately made an alliance with Germany's western neighbor and enemy, France. Wilhelm decided he would charm and manipulate Tsar Nicholas II (a "ninny" and a "whimperer," according to Wilhelm, fit only "to grow turnips") into abandoning the alliance. In 1897, Nicholas told Wilhelm to get lost; the German–Russian alliance withered.

The general staff of the German Army agreed that the Kaiser had neither the attention span nor the ability to lead "three soldiers over a gutter." Wilhelm was "deeply suggestible and would defer to the last person he'd spoken to or cutting he'd read – at least until he'd spoken to the next person … Wilhelm's staff and ministers resorted to manipulation, distraction, and flattery to manage him. 'In order to get him to accept an idea you must act as if the idea were his,' the Kaiser's closest friend, Philipp zu Eulenburg, advised his colleagues, adding, 'Don't forget the sugar.'"

The comparisons are uncanny and mesmerising. But as far as leadership goes, Carter's message is deeply depressing:

> Wilhelm's patronage of the aggressive, nationalistic right left him surrounded by ministers who held a collective conviction that a European war was inevitable and even desirable. Alfred von Tirpitz, Germany's Naval chief – who realized at his first meeting with the Kaiser that he did "not live in the real world" – consciously exploited Wilhelm's envy and rage in order to extract the astronomical sums required to build a German Navy to rival Britain's, a project that created an arms race and became an intractable block to peace negotiations.

Carter's analysis looks to the legacy of the Kaiser, long after he had lost power and authority. She argues:

> Wilhelm's touchiness, his unpredictability, his need to be acknowledged: these things struck a chord with elements in Germany, which was in a kind of adolescent spasm – quick to perceive slights, excited by the idea of flexing its muscles, filled with a sense of entitlement. At the same time, Wilhelm's posturing raised tensions in Europe … Once the war was actually upon him, the government and military effectively swept the Kaiser aside. And the gravest damage occurred only after Wilhelm abdicated, in November of 1918 … The defeated Germany sank into years of depression, resentments sharpened, the toxic lie that Germany had been "robbed" of its rightful victory in the war took hold.

It is worth considering the structural changes to the presidency that will be left behind after Trump has gone.

Between the normalisation of a new sense of executive power, and the US Supreme Court judgment in mid-2018, which effectively means a presidential order can overturn anything, as long as it claims to be done on the grounds of national security, we have reached a very different power balance in the American political system. It is one where the sort of leadership recipe that Heifetz talks about becomes less relevant: a process in which the requirements of balancing and managing the pressures in the political system are reduced, and in which, once a president has won a mandate, he or she can rely on the authority and power of office to do whatever they want. For along the way, the counterweights to executive power have been weakened. As Hugh White observed in his Quarterly Essay *Without America*, this in turn means that "the authority and credibility of the policy establishment is at its weakest when America needs it most."

> It became harder and harder under Bush and Obama for US friends and allies to believe that America was a country whose strength, resolve and statecraft they could rely on. Under Trump it becomes almost impossible ... He seems to have no concept of the state itself as a great collective enterprise with interests and objectives beyond his own. It really is all about him, so he speaks and acts simply for himself, not so much reckless about as quite unconscious of the consequences for the country he is supposed to lead.

Much contemporary commentary in Washington concerns who, if anyone, has the president's ear, and who, if anyone, can direct or control his energies. Trump's White House, with its revolving door of advisers and experts, is not quite the Kaiser's court of military figures all urging him in the one direction. But there are elements of this. There is a battle royale on trade, for example, with an adviser who wrote a book called *Death by China*, Peter Navarro, urging the president to pursue aggressive trade policies, over the objection of others, such as treasury secretary Steven Mnuchin, according to *The New York Times*.

An alternative view of Donald Trump's presidency, from the Centre for Independent Studies' Tom Switzer, urges us to look beyond the horror and chaos of his day-to-day presidency and examine what Trump has done.

> For all the spin and flip-flopping of modern politics, here's a bloke who practises what he preaches. The list is long and growing. He pulled the United States out of the Trans-Pacific Partnership, the Paris climate pact and the Iran nuclear deal. He will move permanently the US embassy in Israel to Jerusalem. He has slashed the US company tax rates and stacked the judiciary with qualified conservatives. He has put a "travel ban" that restricted entry to America from several Muslim nations ... On July 16, Trump will broker detente with Vladimir Putin in Helsinki. For the most part, Trump is doing it his way, keeping America out of Middle East quagmires while playing nice with the Kremlin and Kim regime.

Ronald Heifetz's argument, based on his assessments of other leaders, would be that without both unifying the community behind an issue and having a detached oversight of policy goals, leadership will be flawed and the leader's agenda will ultimately fail.

For now, Trump is giving his supporters what they want. But we are already seeing the price of some of these follies in massive subsidies having to be given to American farmers hurt by his trade war on Europe.

Heifetz argues that the emergence of America's dominant role in twentieth-century world affairs saw the presidency revert "to the imperial mode ... Congress and the public as a whole expected technical expertise and autocratic policymaking in the guise of leadership and that is what they got." But the risk with this approach is that "doubt, the exchange of ideas, weighing contrary values, collaborative work, the testing of vision against competing views, changing one's mind, seem like unaffordable luxuries."

And this is where the real danger of Trump's style of leadership lies. Attacked, he doubles down. If we do not question his approach, we become ever more reliant on it working, but ever less able to influence or challenge it. *Vox* co-founder Matthew Yglesias writes:

> The economy is growing, and American soldiers abroad are not dying in large numbers. We would normally expect a president enjoying those conditions to have pretty good approval ratings. Trump's are terrible.
>
> And it seems plausible to attribute those numbers to the all-base, all-the-time refusal to do anything on either a symbolic or a policy level to try to reassure people who aren't in his base that their worst fears about him are mistaken. Trump's strength with his base, meanwhile, isn't a mitigating factor – it's part of the overall problem. In a divided country, he makes no effort to serve as a unifying figure.

In the Heifetz analysis, Lyndon Johnson made a fatal mistake in foreign policy by acting alone – which meant not taking advice – and surprising not only his enemy, but also American voters.

Did Trump's base expect him to go as far as he has with NATO and have they considered the potential consequences of that, or did they simply believe he was going to talk tough and get better budget commitments from his European allies? His base will stick if there seem to be successes. But he would leave them with no fallbacks if things start to collapse.

We have to consider a leader's legacy, as much as what the leader is doing in the moment. If that means leaving huge, possibly new divisions in the community, and the institutions of democracy weakened and diminished in the eyes of voters, that is only a recipe for larger problems in the future. That is the ultimate failure of leadership.

IS THERE AN ALTERNATIVE?

Around the world, we are seeing the return of the "strongman" – if not necessarily the "great man." We have Vladimir Putin in Russia, Xi Jinping in China, and Recep Tayyip Erdoğan in Turkey, among others, consolidating their power. We were probably deluding ourselves, after the Cold War, that they were going away.

In the United States, Donald Trump is not setting up a totalitarian dictatorship, but the machismo of the leader who will brook no opposition is central to his bizarre and alarming political persona.

It is easy to be alarmist about Trump, but in *How Democracies Die*, Steven Levitsky and Daniel Ziblatt make a compelling case for deterioration in the condition of US democracy. They note that Democrats and Republicans "have become much more than just two competing parties, sorted into liberal and conservative camps. Their voters are now deeply divided by race, religious belief, culture, and geography. Republican politicians from Newt Gingrich to Donald Trump learned that in a polarized society, treating rivals as enemies can be useful – and that the pursuit of politics as warfare can mobilize people who fear they have much to lose." They argue that Trump is not the first would-be demagogue to seek the presidency but the first to escape the boundaries of the US system of checks and balances and be "elected a president with no real allegiance to democratic norms." Elected autocrats subvert democracy, the two men write, by:

> packing and "weaponizing" the courts and other neutral agencies, buying off the media and the private sector (or bullying them into silence), and rewriting the rules of politics to permanently disadvantage their rivals. The tragic paradox of the electoral route to authoritarianism is that democracy's enemies use the very institutions of democracy – gradually, subtly, and even legally – to kill it.

Donald Trump's use of just such weapons is a timely reminder not just of the fragility of democracy, but also of the fact that it remains an aberration in history, and that the relationship between leader and led is often one dictated purely by the leader.

*

In the aftermath of World War II, Europe chose a very different political path to the United States' embrace of increasing presidential authority. Scarred by their immediate experiences of authoritarian power, Europeans gravitated to politics driven by consensus and, in the development of the European Union, to government by bureaucrats.

In his masterly book *Postwar*, historian Tony Judt describes how "as a modest substitute for the defunct ambitions of Europe's ideological past, there emerged belatedly – and largely by accident – the 'European model'":

> a distinctively "European" way of regulating social intercourse and inter-state relations. Embracing everything from child-care to inter-state legal norms, this European approach stood for more than just the bureaucratic practices of the European Union and its member states; by the beginning of the twenty-first century it had become a beacon and example for aspirant EU members and a global challenge to the United States and the competing appeal of the "American way of life."

The new need for consensus, the trend to multi-party coalition governments, as well as the often-unspoken reality of Western European nations' relative decline in global power – all these served to constrain and reshape what was required of European leaders.

Two of the most interesting and important contemporary studies in leadership now are Germany's Angela Merkel – even as she appears to be reaching the end of her long period of dominance – and France's Emmanuel Macron – who is still in the early stages of what looks to be a lengthy stay in power.

While many people outside Germany hailed Merkel in the early days of the Trump era as the new Leader of the Free World, impressions of her at home – even before the immigration crisis of 2015 – were very different. The Germans have turned the chancellor's name into a verb – *merkeln* – that refers to indecision and delay, to failing to have an opinion on something, to over-analysis and procrastination. Her countrymen and women will express their exasperation at Merkel's "lead from behind" style. But she is still referred to as *Mutti* – a familiar form for "mother."

In German politics, Merkel has made an artform of being the last person to speak on an issue. This reflects in part how the chancellor is a creature of circumstance and a product of the particular political system in Germany, where multi-party coalitions – spanning a vast political space – have dominated now for decades. Imagine a government formed by both the Coalition and the Labor Party in Australia, with at various times either the Nationals and One Nation, or at other times the Greens, in positions of dominance and influence beyond their numbers, and you get a sense of the complexities of German political management. This requires a very different set of leadership skills and is framed by very different leadership expectations than the ones that shape our political debate in Australia.

At the same time, this system of coalition-building helped entrench the position of Merkel in the 2017 election campaign, despite the unpopularity of her (uncharacteristic) captain's call on letting a million asylum seekers into Germany in the midst of the great Middle Eastern refugee wave. That decision is often cited in Germany as one of the few times when Merkel did go out in front of the community and challenge it to accept a shift, and consider what as a nation it stood for. But, as she remarked privately to others after the election, her dominance of German politics still meant that, while speculation swirled about which parties she could draw into a coalition, none of them could form a coalition without her.

If we apply the Heifetz model, we see that Merkel's approach reflects a quieter way of successfully leading. She has survived as leader in Germany for over a decade by not leading, in a way. That is, she mastered the art of letting a debate yell itself out until she saw an opportunity, or sensed a need, to intervene and make a declaration about where it would land. She has obliged all her fellow coalition members to clarify their positions and allowed other voices to speak. Merkel herself speaks very little. She gives few interviews. She is not out in the public domain every day addressing the latest controversy, or the latest football result.

In his biography of Merkel, Matthew Qvortrup relates a story of Angela as a small girl in communist East Germany, where teachers were under pressure to identify sporting talent. Merkel's PE teacher suggested she try the three-metre diving board.

> She knew that diving head first into the water could be painful, and the teacher probably expected her to make a jump feet first and then declare that this was not for her. That would save him time ... But Angela always did as she was told. She climbed up the twelve steps, took a hesitant step and peered into the water. It was frightening. She turned back. But she didn't go down. She walked to and fro, analyzing the situation. The other children were amused, and some of the boys started laughing. But Angela continued her analysis. Finally, just as the bell rang to signal that the class was over, she dived head first into the water ... The other pupils didn't laugh; none of them had dived in. Angela did – after she had analysed the situation.

Qvortrup says Merkel, as chancellor, would recall the story of the diving board when her compatriots – and indeed the foreign media – criticised her for being indecisive. Like the girl who did not care what her classmates said, the adult politician was unmoved by criticism. Indeed, she saw hesitancy as a virtue.

> I am quite brave when a decision has to be made. But I need a bit of a run-up and I like – if possible – to think before I jump. I always

> like to know what will happen to me, even if this means that I am less spontaneous.

In mid-2018, having spent months stitching together yet another difficult governing coalition, Merkel faced a crisis when the leader of her main coalition partner, the Bavaria-based CSU, staged a challenge to her position on immigration. There was a new – and, it seemed, very real – chance of her losing the chancellorship. Two factors made this challenge particularly potent. This time, the CSU leader Horst Seehofer was Merkel's interior minister, so could, if he wanted to, set policy himself under the rules of German politics. The second factor was the realpolitik involved: the CSU faced state elections in Bavaria and was under challenge from the far-right anti-immigration party, the Alternative for Germany.

And of course there was a personal element to the challenge. The German magazine *Der Spiegel* reported in July that:

> Seehofer is like an onion: You have to have a bit of patience, but once you peel your way to the center, you'll find Merkel, the woman who has inflicted so many injuries on him and who he has never been able to defeat. Sooner or later, it's always Merkel with him. And he can't help it, it's a mixture of admiration and fear. He is intimately familiar with her instinct for power, which so many before him have underestimated and who thus lie "in the cemetery behind the Chancellery," as Seehofer says. He doesn't want to end up there himself.

Merkel's response was to put off the policy threat from Seehoffer until an EU summit on refugees a few weeks later. A perceptive observer of German politics argued to me that the advantage of this was that it not only bought Merkel time, but also bought her CSU challenger time to modify a hardline position which was as unlikely to prevail as her own. To those of us schooled in the machismo of Australian politics, this observation may cause us to scratch our heads. Why would there be any advantage to Merkel in assisting her challenger? The argument is that Merkel knew her opponent had laid down demands that could never be met in the time frame at hand, and in the political framework of the European Union. He needed a get-out-of-jail card from his own policy, just as she needed some form of compromise, if the crisis was going to be in any way calmed down.

And that was what happened. Merkel returned from the summit with promises from a number of countries, including Greece and Spain, to take back asylum seekers who reached Germany's borders via their territories. Amid a growing backlash against asylum seekers that has been changing the political map in Europe, the summit agreed on measures that sound all too familiar in Australia, but were very new in the EU. There would be controlled centres, where refugees would wait for their asylum applications to be approved or denied. There would be "disembarkation platforms," whence migrants who made their way across the Mediterranean could be shipped back to North Africa. Just how realistic the measures would be was an issue. But for Merkel, they gave her enough to keep her government together and to retain control of the agenda.

A leader's ability to manipulate time in order to gain space both to think and act (and the luck or bad luck that might accompany the timing of decisions) is a crucial part of successful leadership. On this topic, the English writer A.N. Wilson noted that Elizabeth I's advisers and courtiers were always:

> urging her to make decisions; to be Catholic or to be Protestant; to marry; to fight a decisive and expensive war in Ireland or the Low Countries. In almost all cases, Elizabeth had dithered, Hamlet-like; and dithering had been, if not the right policy, then at least not the wrong policy … Elizabeth, like Hamlet, could see the calamitous effects of too great a precision and too great a decisiveness in political life.

John Lewis Gaddis in turn noted that:

> Elizabeth used dithering … to remind her advisers for whom they worked; to hold off her suitors, thus balancing their states; and, when the balance at last turned against her, to lure the Spanish Armada into the English Channel where, by trusting her admirals, she sprang a massive mousetrap.

There are lessons for Australia in considering the Merkel approach, particularly in an era when disillusionment with the major parties is forcing them increasingly into formal or informal coalitions, or reliance on minor parties and independents. The major lesson would be an acceptance of the need for pragmatism, and for compromise. The framework for assessing the minority Gillard government and the near-minority Turnbull government has remained one formed in a time when governments had a much firmer grip on the parliament, and on an agenda. That tends to mean that the pressure is on to answer questions that can't be answered, or for solutions that are simply not possible in the circumstances, and to undervalue compromises when they are made.

*

After the 2017 German elections, with Merkel having to spend months negotiating a coalition, and with the UK convulsed by Brexit, international attention on Europe switched to Emmanuel Macron, Merkel's closest partner in the project to revive and strengthen the European Union in the face of Donald Trump's announced intention to withdraw from European and global affairs.

If Merkel's political leadership style was to lead from behind, Macron's was to lead from the front, the sides and the middle. The former investment banker and bureaucrat came from nowhere to win the French presidential elections in May 2017. Not only did he win the presidency, his new party swept into the French parliament so powerfully that it broke the hold of the traditional major political parties. Macron's La République En Marche!, in alliance with the Democratic Movement, won

350 of the 577 seats in the National Assembly, the lower house of the French parliament. This included an outright majority of 308 seats for Macron's party. The Socialist Party was reduced to 30 seats and the Republicans to 112 seats, the lowest-ever results for the centre-left and centre-right in the legislative elections.

Not that the 39-year-old was offering a populist agenda. He was instead proposing to the notoriously stubborn French a suite of policies aimed at deregulating labour markets and the economy. The Macron biographer Adam Plowright wrote in *The Guardian* six months into his presidency that:

> France, the country of revolution, is once again a leading political laboratory. Macron is the most vivid example yet of a modern-day political disruptor. Not only did he create a victorious party from scratch in record time, he also won with a progressive centrist manifesto at a time of surging rightwing nationalism.

But Macron carried the advantage that the election process had been whittled down to a race between him and the far-right National Front's Marine Le Pen. French voters who were horrified at the prospect of a win by the National Front delivered him a huge victory – and then sullenly resented his reforming zeal. But circumstances had given him the political space to move rapidly once he got into office, a commodity as important as time to think.

In an age when politicians have become cautious, and politics a profession, Macron jumps into debates, not just about France and Europe but about the future of Africa, Asia and the world in general, declaring his ambition to solve the unsolvable. The French president is prone to long speeches – he gave a speech on the future of Europe in late 2017 that went for more than two hours – and high-wire announcements that sound as if they come from an earlier age.

Der Spiegel interviewed him in late 2017 after six months in the presidency and observed that often things work differently in practice than theory. Macron replied:

> That is true. You can anticipate and plan everything, but when you actually experience it, it's different. For me, my office isn't first and foremost a political or technical one. Rather, it is symbolic. I am a strong believer that modern political life must rediscover a sense for symbolism. We need to develop a kind of political heroism. I don't mean that I want to play the hero. But we need to be amenable once again to creating grand narratives. If you like, post-modernism was the worst thing that could have happened to our democracy. The idea that you have to deconstruct and destroy all grand narratives is not a good one. Since then, trust has evaporated in everything and everyone ... Critique is necessary, but where does this hate for the so-called grand narrative come from?
>
> DER SPIEGEL: Why is this narrative so important?
>
> MACRON: I think we need it badly! Why is a portion of our youth so fascinated by extremes, jihadism for example? Why do modern democracies refuse to allow their citizens to dream? Why can't there be such a thing as democratic heroism? Perhaps exactly that is our task: rediscovering something like that together for the twenty-first century.

Macron seems to break all the Heifetz rules about how to approach the job of leader. Like Trump, he wants in his own way to break the system, or drain the swamp, and make France "great again." But he does it without finding scapegoats, with a much clearer purpose and sense of direction about how it should be transformed. In his election manifesto, he said that:

> engaging in politics assumes going beyond thought patterns that are convenient and in some respects comfortable, but which offer nothing beneficial – by which I simply mean whatever may contribute to building a world that is more acceptable and more just.
>
> The political class and the media are a band of sleepwalkers who refuse to see what is coming their way. From time to time they

> express outrage, but without drawing the necessary conclusions …
>
> If we do not bring ourselves to our senses, within five or ten years the National Front will accede to power. There is no longer any doubt about this. We cannot, after each terrorist attack or each election loss, call for national unity, ask the country to make sacrifices, and think that the political class for its part can continue its petty business as usual. That would be a moral misjudgment and a historic wrong.
>
> It is not a question of attacking those who vote for the National Front. I have always considered that to be an error. I know too many French citizens who have voted that way, not out of conviction, but simply to protest against an established order that has forgotten them, or out of pique. We have to touch people's lives. Give them direction and vision, and fight this party that is manipulating their anger.

Emmanuel Macron may have both recognised and benefited from the sweetest spot in Western politics today. He recognised the disaffection with the major political parties and, unlike many who have ridden this wave, has wrangled it into a new political movement with extraordinary success. But his success was buttressed by fear of the alternative – the far right. Electoral success has meant he faces no great challenge from the parliament. He does not need to appease coalition partners. Most significantly, he went to voters with a very clear manifesto which was far from populist, most notably in its proposal to alter French labour laws.

Because he is not a populist, he is not crippled by expectations that he can transform French society. In fact, many voters meet his ambition with trepidation at the pace of change he wishes to set. To much derision, Macron likens himself to Jupiter and often shows a dangerous impatience. He is advocating big change in Africa, in the European Union, even in our region. And he is advocating free trade.

Der Spiegel asked Macron in 2017 about the differences between France and Germany. He replied:

> Germany is different from France. You are more Protestant, which results in a significant difference. Through the church, through Catholicism, French society was structured vertically, from top to bottom. I am convinced that it has remained so until today. That might sound shocking to some – and don't worry, I don't see myself as a king. But whether you like it or not, France's history is unique in Europe. Not to put too fine a point on it, France is a country of regicidal monarchists. It is a paradox: the French want to elect a king, but they would like to be able to overthrow him whenever they want. The office of president is not a normal office – that is something one should understand when one occupies it. You have to be prepared to be disparaged, insulted and mocked – that is in the French nature. And: as president, you cannot have a desire to be loved. Which is, of course, difficult because everybody wants to be loved. But in the end, that's not important. What is important is serving the country and moving it forward.

In his words, we see a clear recognition of the importance of reinvigorating the authority of the office of president. He told voters before the election:

> Today, French citizens have the impression that their government no longer governs. Whether in the matters of Europe, political parties, markets, opinion polls, or the street, there is confusion about who holds power. The government therefore needs to reclaim control, and explain what it is doing, because explanations enable society to accept what is being done.

It will be most fascinating to watch over the coming years whether he can do this without resorting to the sort of strongman persona and tactics that are at the heart of Trump's political identity.

By contrast, Angela Merkel, with her cautious but steely nature, is locked in by tight numbers in the parliament and by a difficult coalition.

She is not buttressed by fear of the alternative, but must keep that alternative at bay. She has been re-elected with very little manifesto other than continuity. But the German political debate, much more than is the case in English-speaking democracies, is conducted in civil terms, and Merkel's dominance over national politics has earned a respect which means the authority of the chancellor's office has largely been maintained.

*

In a famous essay, Max Weber argued that "devotion to the charisma of the prophet, or the leader in war, or to the great demagogue in the ecclesia or in parliament, means that the leader is personally recognized as the innerly 'called' leader of men":

> Men do not obey him by virtue of tradition or statute, but because they believe in him. If he is more than a narrow and vain upstart of the moment, the leader lives for his cause and "strives for his work." The devotion of his disciples, his followers, his personal party friends is oriented to his person and to its qualities. Charismatic leadership has emerged in all places and in all historical epochs.
>
> Most importantly in the past, it has emerged in the two figures of the magician and the prophet on the one hand, and in the elected warlord, the gang leader and *condottiere* on the other hand.

We certainly don't obey our leaders in Australia, and we do not defer to them by "virtue of tradition or statute." But I think we have increasingly sought the magician and the prophet.

That yearning for the magician or the prophet has not been unique to Australia. As Jeff Shesol wrote, Americans are always looking for the "great man" too. In some countries that yearning has shifted from the prophet to the elected warlord.

There are many lessons in these brief portraits: the different ways politicians can use the powers at their disposal; that leadership can vary with the nature of the political system in a democracy; that factors other than charisma help determine what leaders are capable of – factors that shore up voter support (in the case of Macron, as a bulwark against the far right). More than anything, applied to Australian political discussion, these portraits challenge the idea that the personal will, qualities and charisma of a leader necessarily define leadership.

It is a freezing day in Seattle in 1993. Paul Keating is touring the massive Boeing factory while he is in the north-western American city for the first ever APEC heads of government meeting, an initiative largely of his making, which he has persuaded US President Bill Clinton to champion as the first host. At a doorstop interview on the factory floor, he is asked about the one leader from the region who has declined to attend, Malaysia's Mahathir Mohamad. His response causes uproar.

> Please don't ask me any more questions about Dr Mahathir. I couldn't care less, frankly, whether he comes or not ... Malaysia is a country which Australia has interests with, and which is a neighbour, and I'll see him on those terms. But APEC is bigger than all of us: Australia, the US and Malaysia and Dr Mahathir and any other recalcitrants.

The uproar around the "recalcitrant" comment, and the APEC leaders' summit more broadly, marked a turning point in the way Australia conducted itself on the world stage.

As treasurer, Keating had long chafed at the lack of a forum in which Australia could have its voice heard. The Group of Six – later Seven (G7) – had developed in the 1970s and '80s, and billed itself as a meeting of the major industrialised countries, the world's economic powerhouses. It had the capacity to set international economic policy. Long before the global financial crisis helped clear the way for the G20 – which finally saw Australia, China and India invited into the conversation after persistent lobbying by Kevin Rudd – APEC was our entry into regional and international discussions. It also heralded an era of international summits, which now take up a significant part of an Australian prime minister's calendar in the second half of each year.

While the APEC agenda – which started life focused on free trade – has become somewhat obscure, the significance of the international summit season is that it has changed the way our leaders interact with others around the world. Thirty years ago, an Australian prime minister might go to the United States once, perhaps twice, in a parliamentary term, and might also travel to Japan or the UK. The expectations that built up around those meetings and, as a result, the perceptions of whether the prime minister had been "successful," were important at home. The prime minister was dealing with another international leader, whom he probably didn't know very well, in a highly institutionalised setting. Hence, the Australian cringe was invariably in full swing: was the prime minister going to make a gauche goose of himself and embarrass the rest of us?

Today, though, Australian prime ministers are expected to have positions on world events and press them hard, not confining themselves to the immediate matter of the bilateral relationship. That changes the way we see and judge our leaders. Australian leaders no longer just have a broad in-principle position on a global development that has no direct bearing on us, but are expected to comment on all the daily developing nuances, from Syria and Ukraine to the relationship between Britain and the European Union. Foreign policy is now an ever-encroaching, day-to-day issue in Australian politics. In the past, it dominated in times of intense conflict or war, but otherwise faded into the background of domestic concerns.

Yet the forces that drive the debate on foreign policy, and the people who shape it, are completely different from the pressures and players that drive the domestic agenda. Showing leadership on an international issue effectively means impressing your peers in other countries. The authority with which you act has completely different sources to the ones at home.

Globalisation has transformed the influence of the rest of the world on our country and reduced political leaders' scope to act. Consider an issue like the mass movement of people around the world and how it has seemingly ultimately overpowered the savviest of leaders, no matter what approach they take to the issue. As we saw in the movement of people from Syria to Europe in 2015, everyone was reliant on everyone else to find a solution. Europe's lack of internal borders may have made the problem more dramatic, but the million people who fled north would still have had to go somewhere. And the capacity of neighbouring countries to act independently of each other would still have been negligible.

Similarly, the most consistent argument in support of the Coalition's push to cut company tax rates in the past couple of years has been the need to keep Australia's business environment competitive with other countries', to ensure we attract businesses and investment.

We have become much more exposed to such pressures. And of course we are now dealing with a much more complicated world. It is no longer the world split in two of the Cold War era. It is too simple to say it is a world divided between the United States and China. Beyond superpower plays, the old global systems and multilateral structures that have dominated most of our lifetimes are under full-scale assault. The world is awash not just with protectionist sentiment, but also with larger-than-life political leaders who must be dealt with outside the standard terms of their national interest versus ours.

These linked changes – the rise of strongmen leaders, the decline of Western alliances and the breakdown of multilateralism – are now happening at breakneck speed, requiring much more of Australia and its political leaders than the day-to-day discussion of our relationships with the United States and China would suggest.

We need our leader not just to run a delicate line between the US and China, but to try to shore up, and reinvent, a role for Australia as one of a handful of middle powers that remain advocates for the international order – even perhaps to make a judgment that that order is over and imagine what the new one will look like.

We might keep our alliance with the US and juggle this with our economically dependent relationship with China. But beyond the debate over how we manage these two giants is the reality that both our historical major alliance partners – Britain and the United States – are now inwardly focused when it comes to policy and distracted by the sheer drama of their internal politics. There has never been a starker demonstration of why we have to work out who we are in the world by ourselves.

The view that we are a "middle power," with both limitations and capabilities, doesn't often feature in our discussion. Yet it should be shaping the way we think about foreign policy and how our leaders project us in the world: how we can turn our middle-power status into an asset, and make the most of it. This might change the way we see ourselves and the possibilities we have for making alliances with other middle powers, in our region and beyond.

Other countries are also grappling with these issues. Consider how both Germany and France, and the European Union collectively, have been trying to adapt to this new world. Despite all the criticism of the stodginess of the EU and NATO, defence policy there has moved conspicuously further in the last four years than in Australia. Even before the arrival of Trump, increasing military aggression by Russia and terror attacks in European cities forced European leaders to consider greater defence and security cooperation for the first time. There are big differences between Western and Eastern Europe on strategic questions, particularly when it comes to Russia. Yet structures are gradually being put in place that allow for some centralisation of command. Negotiations are underway that would allow different countries to move their troops across the EU quickly. Take a step back and consider what an extraordinary transformation this is from a century ago. The Europeans are now racing to upgrade their defences, not from each other, but from external threats.

Having to deal with strongmen, rather than other leaders who also advocate for the international order, changes what is required of leaders, as do the difficulties of dealing with such strongmen when they behave erratically. These pressures were revealed to us in the leaked transcript of Malcolm Turnbull's first phone call with the incoming US president early last year.

How many times do we get to read a transcript of a conversation between two national leaders, let alone one that involves an erratic and spectacularly ill-informed president of the United States? It was a fascinating lesson in realpolitik: Turnbull continually trying to bring Trump back to the subject at hand, cajoling, revealing, insisting, humouring ...whatever it took to keep the conversation on track in a relationship where Australia didn't have too many cards in its hand. It also gave one of the few real insights into how leaders place policy in the context of politics, and a demonstration of the quandaries that arise when dealing with a figure such as Trump. And for that reason, it is worth quoting in full:

Prime Minister Malcolm Turnbull (MT): Good evening.

President Donald Trump (DT): Mr Prime Minister, how are you?

MT I am doing very well.

DT And I guess our friend Greg Norman, he is doing very well?

MT He is a great mutual friend, yes.

DT Well, you say hello to him. He is a very good friend. By the way, thank you very much for taking the call. I really appreciate it. It is really nice.

MT Thank you very much. Everything is going very well. I want to congratulate you and Mike Pence on being sworn in now. I have spoken to you both now, as you know. I know we are both looking to make our relationship, which is very strong and intimate, stronger than ever – which I believe we can do.

DT Good.

MT I believe you and I have similar backgrounds, unusual for politicians, more businessman [sic] but I look forward to working together.

DT That is exactly right. We do have similar backgrounds and it seems to be working in this climate – it is a crazy climate. Let me tell you this, it is an evil time but it is a complex time because we do not have uniforms standing in front of us. Instead, we have people in disguise. It is brutal. This ISIS thing – it is something we are going to devote a lot of energy to it. I think we are going to be very successful.

MT Absolutely. We have, as you know, taken a very strong line on national security and border protection here and when I was speaking with Jared Kushner just the other day and one of your immigration advisers in the White House we reflected on how our policies have helped to inform your approach. We are very much of the same mind. It is very interesting to know how you prioritise the minorities in your executive order. This is exactly what we have done with the program to bring in 12,000 Syrian refugees, 90 per cent of which will be Christians. It will be quite deliberate and the position I have taken – I have been very open about it – is that it is a tragic fact of life that when the situation in the Middle East settles down – the people that are going to be most unlikely to have a continuing home are those Christian minorities. We have seen that in Iraq and so from our point of view, as a final destination for refugees, that is why we prioritise. It is not a sectarian thing. It is recognition of the practical political realities. We have a similar perspective in that respect.

DT Do you know four years ago, Malcolm, I was with a man who does this for a living. He was telling me, before the migration, that if you were a Christian from Syria, you had no chance of coming to the United States. Zero. They were the ones being persecuted. When I say persecuted, I mean their heads were being chopped off. If you were a Muslim – we have nothing against Muslims – but if you were a Muslim, you were not persecuted at least to the extent – but if you were a Muslim from Syria that was the number one place to get into the United States from. That was the easiest thing. But if you were a Christian from Syria you have no chance of getting into the United States. I just thought it was an incredible statistic. Totally true – and you have seen the same thing. It is incredible.

MT Well, yes. Mr President, can I return to the issue of the resettlement agreement that we had with the Obama administration with respect to some people on Nauru and Manus Island. I have written to you about this and Mike Pence and General Flynn spoke with Julie Bishop and my national security adviser yesterday. This is a very big issue for us, particularly domestically, and I do understand you are inclined to a different point of view than the vice president.

DT Well, actually, I just called for a total ban on Syria and from many different countries from where there is terror, and extreme vetting for everyone else – and somebody told me yesterday that close to 2000 people are coming who are really probably troublesome. And I am saying, boy, that will make us look awfully bad. Here I am calling for a ban where I am not letting anybody in and we take 2000 people. Really it looks like 2000 people that Australia does not want, and I do not blame you by the way, but the United States has become like a dumping ground. You know, Malcolm, anybody that has a problem – you remember the Mariel boat lift, where Castro let everyone out of prison and Jimmy Carter accepted them with open arms. These were brutal people. Nobody said Castro was stupid, but now what are we talking about is 2000 people that are actually imprisoned and that would actually come into the United States. I heard about this – I have to say I love Australia; I love the people of Australia. I have so many friends from Australia, but I said – geez, that is a big ask, especially in light of the fact that we are so heavily in favour, not in favour, but we have no choice but to stop things. We have to stop. We have allowed so many people into our country that should not be here. We have our San Bernardinos, we have had the World Trade Center come down because of people that should not have been in our country, and now we are supposed to take 2000. It sends such a bad signal. You have no idea. It is such a bad thing.

MT Can you hear me out, Mr President?

DT Yeah, go ahead.

MT Yes, the agreement, which the vice president just called the foreign minister about less than twenty-four hours ago and said your administration would be continuing, does not require you to take 2000 people. It does not require you to take any. It requires, in return, for us to do a number of things for the United States – this is a big deal, I think we should respect deals.

DT Who made the deal? Obama?

MT Yes, but let me describe what it is. I think it is quite consistent. I think you can comply with it. It is absolutely consistent with your executive order, so please just hear me out. The obligation is for the United States to look and examine and take up to and only if they so choose – 1250 to 2000. Every individual is subject to your vetting. You can decide to take them or to not take them after vetting. You can decide to take 1000 or 100. It is entirely up to you. The obligation is to only go through the process. So that is the first thing. Secondly, the people – none of these people are from the conflict zone. They are basically economic refugees from Iran, Pakistan, and Afghanistan. That is the vast bulk of them. They have been under our supervision for over three years now and we know exactly everything about them.

DT Why haven't you let them out? Why have you not let them into your society?

MT Okay, I will explain why. It is not because they are bad people. It is because in order to stop people smugglers, we had to deprive them of the product. So we said if you try to come to Australia by boat, even if we think you are the best person in the world, even if you are a Nobel Prize–winning genius, we will not let you in. Because the problem with the people –

DT That is a good idea. We should do that too. You are worse than I am.

MT This is our experience.

DT Because you do not want to destroy your country. Look at what has happened in Germany. Look at what is happening in these countries. These people are crazy to let this happen. I spoke to Merkel today, and believe me, she wishes she did not do it. Germany is a mess because of what happened.

MT I agree with you, letting one million Syrians walk into their country. It was one of the big factors in the Brexit vote, frankly.

DT Well, there could be two million people coming in Germany. Two million people. Can you believe it? It will never be the same.

MT I stood up at the UN in September and set up what our immigration policy was. I said that you cannot maintain popular support for immigration policy, multiculturalism, unless you can control your borders. The bottom line is that we got here. I am asking you as a very good friend. This is a big deal. It is really, really important to us that we maintain it. It does not oblige you to take one person that you do not want. As I have said, your homeland officials have visited and they have already interviewed these people. You can decide. It is at your discretion. So you have the wording in the Executive Order that enables the Secretary of Homeland Security and the Secretary of State to admit people on a case-by-case basis in order to conform with an existing agreement. I do believe that you will never find a better friend to the United States than Australia. I say this to you sincerely that it is in the mutual interest of the United States to say, "Yes, we can conform with that deal – we are not obliged to take anybody we do not want, we will go through extreme vetting," and that way you are seen to show the respect that a trusted ally wants and deserves. We will then hold up our end of the bargain by taking in our country thirty-one [*inaudible*] that you need to move on from.

DT Malcolm, why is this so important? I do not understand. This is going to kill me. I am the world's greatest person that does not want to let people into the country. And now I am agreeing to take 2000 people and I agree I can vet them, but that puts me in a bad position. It makes me look so bad and I have only been here a week.

MT With great respect, that is not right – it is not 2000.

DT Well, it is close. I have also heard like 5000 as well.

MT The given number in the agreement is 1250 and it is entirely a matter of your vetting. I think that what you could say is that [the deal with] the Australian government is consistent with the principles set out in the executive order.

DT No, I do not want [to] say that. I will just have to say that unfortunately I will have to live with what was said by Obama. I will say I hate it. Look, I spoke to Putin, Merkel, Abe of Japan, to France today, and this was my most unpleasant call because I will be honest with you. I hate taking these people. I guarantee you they are bad. That is why they are in prison right now. They are not going to be wonderful people who go on to work for the local milk people.

MT I would not be so sure about that. They are basically –

DT Well, maybe you should let them out of prison. I am doing this because Obama made a bad deal. I am not doing this because it fits into my Executive Order. I am taking 2000 people from Australia who are in prison and the day before I signed an executive order saying that we are not taking anybody in. We are not taking anybody in, those days are over.

MT But can I say to you, there is nothing more important in business or politics than a deal is a deal. Look, you and I have a lot of mutual friends.

DT Look, I do not know how you got them to sign a deal like this, but that is how they lost the election. They said I had no way to 270 and I got 306. That is why they lost the election, because of stupid deals like this. You have brokered many a stupid deal in business and I respect you, but I guarantee that you broke [sic] many a stupid deal. This is a stupid deal. This deal will make me look terrible.

MT Mr President, I think this will make you look like a man who stands by the commitments of the United States. It shows that you are a committed –

DT Okay, this shows me to be a dope. I am not like this but, if I have to do it, I will do it but I do not like this at all. I will be honest with you. Not even a little bit. I think it is ridiculous and Obama should have never signed it. The only reason I will take them is because I have to honour a deal signed by my predecessor and it was a rotten deal. I say that it was a stupid deal like all the other deals that this country signed. You have to see what I am doing. I am unlocking deals that were made by people, these people were incompetent. I am not going to say that it fits within the realm of my Executive Order. We are going to allow 2000 prisoners to come into our country and it is within the realm of my Executive Order? If that is the case, my Executive Order does not mean anything, Malcolm. I look like a dope. The only way that I can do this is to say that my predecessor made a deal and I have no option than to honour the deal. I hate having to do it, but I am still going to vet them very closely. Suppose I vet them closely and I do not take any?

MT That is the point I have been trying to make.

DT How does that help you?

MT Well, we assume that we will act in good faith.

DT Does anybody know who these people are? Who are they? Where do they come from? Are they going to become the Boston bomber in five years? Or two years? Who are these people?

MT Let me explain. We know exactly who they are. They have been on Nauru or Manus for over three years and the only reason we cannot let them into Australia is because of our commitment to not allow people to come by boat. Otherwise we would have let them in. If they had arrived by airplane and with a tourist visa then they would be here.

DT Malcolm, but they are arrived [sic] on a boat?

MT Correct, we have stopped the boats.

DT Give them to the United States. We are like a dumping ground for the rest of the world. I have been here for a period of time, I just want this to stop. I look so foolish doing this. It [sic] know it is good for you but it is bad for me. It is horrible for me. This is what I am trying to stop. I do not want to have more San Bernardinos or World Trade Centers. I could name thirty others, but I do not have enough time.

MT These guys are not in that league. They are economic refugees.

DT Okay, good. Can Australia give me a guarantee that if we have any problems – you know that is what they said about the Boston bombers. They said they were wonderful young men.

MT They were Russians. They were not from any of these countries.

DT They were from wherever they were.

MT Please, if we can agree to stick to the deal, you have complete discretion in terms of a security assessment. The numbers are not 2000 but 1250 to start. Basically, we are taking people from the previous administration that they were very keen on getting out of the United States. We will take more. We will take anyone that you want us to take. The only people that we do not take are people who come by boat. So we would rather take a not very attractive guy that help you out [sic] than to take a Nobel Peace Prize–winner that comes by boat. That is the point.

DT What is the thing with boats? Why do you discriminate against boats? No, I know, they come from certain regions. I get it.

MT No, let me explain why. The problem with the boats is that you are basically outsourcing your immigration program to people smugglers and also you get thousands of people drowning at sea. So what we say is, we will decide which people get to come to Australia who are refugees, economic migrants, businessmen, whatever. We decide. That is our decision. We are a generous multicultural immigration nation like the United States but the government decides, the people's representatives decide. So that is the point. I am a highly transactional businessman like you and I know the deal has to work for both sides. Now Obama thought this deal worked for him and he drove a hard bargain with us – that it was agreed with Obama more than a year ago in the Oval Office, long before the election. The principles of the deal were agreed to.

DT I do not know what he got out of it. We never get anything out of it – START Treaty, the Iran deal. I do not know where they find these people to make these stupid deals. I am going to get killed on this thing.

MT You will not.

DT Yes, I will be seen as a weak and ineffective leader in my first week by these people. This is a killer.

MT You can certainly say that it was not a deal that you would have done, but you are going to stick with it.

DT I have no choice to say that about it. Malcolm, I am going to say that I have no choice but to honour my predecessor's deal. I think it is a horrible deal, a disgusting deal that I would have never made. It is an embarrassment to the United States of America and you can say it just the way I said it. I will say it just that way. As far as I am concerned that is enough, Malcolm. I have had it. I have been making these calls all day and this is the most unpleasant call all day. Putin was a pleasant call. This is ridiculous.

MT Do you want to talk about Syria and DPRK?

DT [*inaudible*] this is crazy.

MT Thank you for your commitment. It is very important to us.

DT It is important to you and it is embarrassing to me. It is an embarrassment to me, but at least I got you off the hook. So you put me back on the hook.

MT You can count on me. I will be there again and again.

DT I hope so. Okay, thank you, Malcolm.

MT Okay, thank you.

In this exchange, we see all the usual presumptions about a conversation between national leaders overturned. It is not usual for a country's leader to speak with one of their closest allies without having been briefed, or else having not read the brief, on the issue to be discussed. It is not usual for a world leader to threaten to abandon a deal with an ally simply because it was signed by his predecessor. And it is certainly not usual for a world leader to say that he is prepared to turn his back on a deal because it will "make me look terrible."

The conversation illustrates in stark terms how Trump – who assesses every issue on whether it will make him look good – twists the processes of government and relationships between states. You sense the conversation finally turning Turnbull's way when he suggests to the president that by sticking to the deal Trump would be seen as a man who stands by commitments; but Turnbull has resorted to flattery rather than rationality to seal the deal.

And the conversation only took place because a golfer – Greg Norman – had been asked to make contact with Trump on behalf of the Australian government.

The net result was that Turnbull got the outcome he wanted from the call, an outcome that was politically crucial to him, both for his asylum-seeker policy and his personal credibility. But it was also a significant conversation for establishing a base from which Australia's relationship with Trump would progress. This first conversation between the president and the prime minister had recorded the significance of the alliance between the two countries in a way that appeared to influence a president who has subsequently shown very little regard for such niceties as alliances.

To date, Australia has fared better than many close American allies, particularly in winning the argument with Washington about why we should be protected from Trump's punitive steel and aluminium tariffs.

There has been a cost, of course. In this era of protectionism, Australian rhetoric in support of free trade has become quieter. The government argues that it is promoting the cause, rather than just talking about it, by pursuing the Trans-Pacific Partnership and a number of free-trade agreements. But the days when we were a vocal advocate of free trade seem to have passed. The government has also been notably silent – when other countries have not – on controversial Trump foreign policy moves, particularly on Israel.

The Trump conversation reveals the brittle hold that formal channels of diplomacy have on our international relations when confronted with a politician who has no interest in such things. Trump's main concern was what the deal might do for his reputation, and on the back of this concern we are transported back to the days of Elizabeth I and Philip II, when so much rested on the figurehead of the state.

Trump's extraordinary and erratic meeting with NATO leaders in July 2018, followed by the disaster of his visit to the United Kingdom, also highlight the dilemmas and confusion he causes other world leaders and countries. How do you respond to a leader who has publicly endorsed one mutually agreed position, but then goes out and disavows it? How do you respond to a leader who, while a guest in your country – in fact, your guest at dinner – does an interview in which he breaks all the rules by commenting on your country's fraught internal politics and even attacks your running of the country, as Trump did to Britain's Theresa May? Normal civilities mean – as they did in these cases – that other leaders brush over such embarrassments, even dismiss them as unimportant. After all, whatever the implications of Trump behaving badly, responding could mean converting his bad behaviour into a full-blown diplomatic incident.

Watch what happened around these two 2018 events and you start to understand why, in history, there has been a slow-motion response to the rise of dangerous world leaders, something that may seem inexplicable to later observers. The reality is that, at the time, no one can quite believe what is happening or know where it is going. As Paul Ham observed, "we demand linear correctness in the lives of politicians and leaders even as we ourselves act in inconsistent and contrarian ways."

Even when people do recognise that the unprecedented is occurring, it is so outside the boundaries of how leaders should behave that no one is quite sure what to do about it. At some point, though, leaders may decide that the actions of a strongman which are not in their own country's interest must be repudiated, in the full knowledge that this is likely to elicit an even more unpredictable response.

At the time of writing, just what Australia might do in these circumstances is not clear, even in the highest echelons of our government and policy institutions.

In the wake of Trump's behaviour in July, John Howard argued that the world had to let him make mistakes: "I thought he was wrong to have said what he did, but he's now dealt with that and the important thing is to understand that people shouldn't take sides too much on Mr Trump." The comments seemed to reflect a reluctance in Australian political circles ever to criticise America. Perhaps if the world holds up a mirror to the US president that reflects his weakness, rather than his strength, it may give him cause to change his behaviour.

The gambles involved in foreign policy are now escalating for our national leaders, which is a great change (outside times of war, of course). For a long time in Australia, the need to maintain foreign relationships, particularly with the United States, has been used to assert the correctness of a particular policy path at home.

John Howard was a master of using the significant crises of his time as prime minister to appear both a man of steel and a leader who would act decisively based on information unavailable to us. Of course, in the case of the Iraq War, it turned out that the information was completely dodgy. But challenging it required caution from other politicians, since it appeared to have the authority not simply of another politician, but of the national security institutions. And Howard was just one of several prime ministers who fought any attempt by the parliament to have a debate on going to war.

Australia's foreign interests have often been seen primarily through the lens of defence policy. "Is someone going to nuke or invade us? We can't afford to get the Americans offside, even if they are in decline." But what of other central tenets of Australian international policy, such as free trade? The arrival of Donald Trump has shaken our politicians and policy-makers out of any slumbering inclination to leave the steering of foreign policy to the United States, as we have often done in the past.

Just as dealing with Donald Trump sets new personal challenges for our political leaders, so too does finding the right language and stance for dealing with strongman Xi Jinping, as opposed to the collective Chinese leadership that has guided China since the revolution. While there is an almost eerie silence about what, if anything, we need to do, or can do, about Trump, the question of how we deal with China is hotly contested by policy analysts. Chinese interference in our country is dismissed by some, and regarded as paranoid fantasy by others, such as the former NSW premier Bob Carr. Writers like Hugh White diagnose a failure to confront reality, based on a false presumption that we will be protected by an American sphere of influence in the Pacific.

The differences between domestic and international leadership seem only to have grown in recent years. In foreign policy, your audience and your voters are not just those who turn up on polling day. Your audience includes other leaders with their own domestic problems, viewing any tricks you pull pragmatically, as practitioners – the very same tricks that might provoke howls of outrage from people at home expecting perfect outcomes.

For the local audience, the practice of foreign policy is not quite so wrapped in mystery and gee-whiz meetings behind closed doors as it was in the past. A leaked full transcript of a private conversation may still be a one-off, but we have become more accustomed to seeing our leaders doing the humdrum work of foreign meetings. Yet while globalisation means the world intrudes more than ever into our national fortunes, foreign policy remains a very different discussion than the domestic agenda. Not only are the issues different, so too are the participants: this is an area where the public still defers to "experts." Let's face it, most of us don't really know that much about China and how it conducts its international relations, or what to make of Europe and Brexit.

The way the politics is handled is different: in many areas of foreign policy, there is a polite and respectful bipartisanship. In times of crisis, the prime minister takes on the mantle of commander-in-chief. There is still the sense – increasingly rare elsewhere – that the government may know more than the rest of us.

The question is whether this disjuncture will persist. Modern communications are breaking down the information monopoly in foreign policy, as they already have in domestic policy. Indonesia's former foreign minister Marty Natalegawa calls this a welcome "democratisation of foreign policy." Issues now abound which have traditionally been viewed as internal but that have:

> foreign policy or external dimensions – food security, energy security, the environment, the management of the economy, migration and the flow refugees, health, terrorism, to cite a few – all defying national solutions alone. Thus, any attempt to promote a democratically obtained mandate at the national level on such issues ultimately requires and demands cooperative partnership across nations.

Diplomacy and foreign policy cannot be the exclusive preserve of a few, Natalegawa argued in a speech in Australia last year. There is:

> the critical need to promote a sense of public participation and ownership for the effective discharge of foreign policies. In a democracy, the conduct of diplomacy and foreign policy, like other fields of government endeavour, cannot be divorced from the public at large ... [there are] wide-ranging constituencies, in particular civil societies, which need to be brought on board ... Foreign policy is always bound to be restrictive in the sense that decisions have to be made by decision-makers – it can't be like a mass decision by everyone unless we began to adopt a referendum for every issue

> that comes to mind – but at the same time leaders need to ensure that the issues being discussed are of relevance to the public at large. That's the major challenge, I think.

As Heifetz highlights, leaders must be consensus-builders. I am arguing here that, like Lyndon Johnson, many of our political leaders have in the past used foreign policy to escape the obligation to consult and build a consensus – whether to pursue actions they believed in on the world stage, or to present themselves as strong leaders at home. It is a melancholy truth that few world leaders today are looking to be consensus-builders. Yet a key task for this generation of Australian political leaders will be to find a path through complex global affairs and build a consensus on – or at least foster an understanding of – a very different self-image for Australia.

That self-image will almost inevitably have to be one that is much more independent, much less fixated on the push and pull of the US–China relationship, and more focused on links in our region and with those powers hoping to retain the multilateralism that has run our world since 1945. Or it may be that a leader emerges who accepts the argument increasingly made that the old order has passed and new ways have to be found of doing business in the world. Either way, our leaders will need to identify this for us, and its implications for our future.

The World Cup game between Australia and Denmark was broadcast late in the evening in Australia and didn't finish until well into the small hours. Malcolm Turnbull was among many Australians watching. Soccer was probably not the prime minister's football code of choice. And he had media interviews lined up the next morning which he could hardly cancel: it had been one of the government's most successful weeks. The Senate had passed a package of personal income tax cuts. But he told a colleague that he couldn't afford not to watch the game. If he was asked about it and relied on a briefing from staff in the morning, he would stuff up and sound like a fraud. Besides, he had to ring and congratulate the team. "They've got to beat Peru now," Turnbull told Melbourne radio host Neil Mitchell the next morning, "but, you know, they are definitely in the hunt!"

> I think they did well, I thought they should have won, but I would say that, wouldn't I, because I'm Australian. But they had more than half of the possession in the game, so there it is, you know – that's football, isn't it? He's a great guy, Mile. I said to him, I said he and Bachar Houli have got the two best-known beards in football, and he gallantly said he thought Bachar put more effort into his beard.

Life was easier for prime ministers when Australia was addicted to fewer sporting codes. And when we didn't expect our prime ministers to follow them all. Everyone knew that Paul Keating had ratcheted up his leadership campaign against Bob Hawke when, though a Sydney boy, he developed an interest in the Collingwood Football Club. But no one ever believed him. Even about the code that had dominated Sydney during his lifetime, rugby league, he could never quite sound convincing. He famously once congratulated a retiring league great who had "kicked a lot of tries for Balmain." And as prime minister he once obliviously walked past Allan Border and members of the Australian cricket team in a hotel foyer in Perth. But no one really cared much. They had a laugh at his expense. His caricature as a lover of French clocks grounded him more in people's minds. It might be bit toffy for a Labor leader, but it was obviously a real interest.

The trivia of life has become such an impediment to political leaders: did Turnbull ever get over having worn a leather jacket on *Q&A* and what that said to voters, who later came to believe he was not the man they thought he was?

It seems we can't even get to the starting gates on the question of judging our leaders these days, because we are bridling at the authenticity question. In the former prime minister's case, he took to the problem by adopting an FM radio strategy – doing interviews with people with names like Woppo and Banger, trying to reveal himself as a real person. The argument is that FM radio is one of the few mass media forums left where politicians can appeal to swinging voters – people who aren't interested enough in politics to tune into the ABC, or who are so entrenched in their views that they listen to the shock jocks, or who might not listen to news bulletins at all. He was certainly not the first leader to go down the FM path. But the fact he felt he had to adopt it as a central plank of his media strategy says how difficult the battle to reach voters has become for politicians in an era of fragmenting media platforms.

Shorten is out there too. He will do radio in the towns and cities he visits. What he will not do is a major print interview. Other than an interview with the men's magazine *GQ*, he hasn't done one, with a major metropolitan newspaper, in years. Somehow, he has got away with this. The Opposition leader plods on in his own fashion, making a virtue of his "town hall"–style meetings around the country as a return to old-fashioned, and real, connection with voters.

All the effort that goes into authenticity comes at a time of great disillusionment and disengagement among voters. This came across in the five 2018 "Super Saturday" by-elections of 28 July. These were universally framed in national terms and as a leadership popularity contest. The prime minister – clearly expecting to win the contest – said the by-elections would be a competition between him and Bill Shorten, one of those great Turnbull gaffes like "and the court will so find" that will always haunt him.

In the Queensland seat of Longman, the only electorate that saw a big change, the swing went against the Coalition – on the primary vote, it was a massive swing of almost 10 per cent. If the by-election was indeed a contest between Turnbull and Shorten, the implications were clear. While the Liberal National Party was humiliated, Labor surprised even itself by lifting its primary vote by 4.5 per cent, and the overall result was disrupted by One Nation's 16 per cent of the primary vote, an increase of 6.5 per cent.

This rebuff of the government in Queensland caused considerable alarm in Coalition ranks, because it has to hold so many marginal seats in the north at the next general election. Something significant was clearly going to have to be done, both to improve the government's stocks and about the underlying damage being inflicted on its vote by One Nation.

There were other important lessons from Super Saturday. In the seat of Braddon in Tasmania, both major parties saw swings against them, as an independent, Craig Garland, running on a classic protest ticket, garnered over 10 per cent of the vote. In the South Australian seat of Mayo, Centre Alliance's Rebekha Sharkie entrenched her hold on the seat over the Liberals. Suffering a 7.5 per cent swing against it, Labor scored a humiliating 6 per cent of the primary vote. In other words, votes were spraying in all directions away from the major parties in Longman, Braddon and Mayo. (In the two Western Australian seats, the Coalition didn't contest, leaving these as a contest between Labor and the Greens.)

Afterwards, there was much criticism of the media for portraying the by-elections as simply a test for Shorten and for "getting it wrong." It was not wrong to observe that Labor held four of the five seats and that, given the historical record on by-elections in Opposition seats, it would have been very damaging for Shorten had Labor lost any of these. But the focus on him did colour much of the national coverage, even if it had little impact on the ground. In Longman, for example, Shorten's face mainly appeared in the Coalition's campaign material, not Labor's. The Coalition believed Shorten was its greatest asset because polling consistently shows him as not liked by voters. This polling lulled the Coalition into a false sense of security and too much negative campaigning. But the Opposition leader was not the swing factor in the Longman by-election. It is not clear Turnbull was the swing factor either, even if pollsters told us he was disliked in Queensland more than in other parts of the country.

All the focus on the leaders meant the swings to minor parties and independents weren't really considered in their own right, as they might once have been. What is important about this trend is that, while the US has channelled its disillusionment into the unlikely figure of Donald Trump – a strongman leader – Australians have channelled their disillusionment into a splintering of the major-party vote. (The only minor party that seems to have been going backwards in recent times is the Greens.)

The splintering of the vote in the July by-elections contained no clear shift to the left and the right, but instead was a failure to win the centre. As election analyst Tim Colebatch wrote in *Inside Story*:

> It is sad to see Turnbull, who once stood for something better, engaging in gutter politics, avoiding any hard decisions – especially on climate change, where his government has now effectively abandoned Australia's pledge under the Paris agreement – and relying on rosy forecasting to hide the still-parlous state of the budget the Coalition had promised to fix. Malcolm, if I may, one piece of advice. The people you have lost are broadly those in the political centre. They are looking for the values you promised to bring to politics: adult conversation about issues; an end to mud-slinging and personal attacks on opponents; respect for truth and objective facts; respect for people; and willingness to look ahead, plan for the long term and explain the issues to voters. That is the new politics they thought you would bring to replace the thirty years of leaders who tried to divide us and rule. The election must be held by May. You have nine months to regain the goodwill you have squandered since 2015.

For conservative agitators in the Coalition, however, the vote in Longman represented something else. It was confirmation that the Coalition was losing its base to One Nation and that it had to move to capture it back.

This meant a shift to the right, and to a world where the lowest common denominator of populist politics would more conspicuously wag the national agenda – an ugly, Trump-like world of race-baiting politics with implications far beyond climate change policy.

When this was combined with a very personal campaign by Tony Abbott and a handful of colleagues to wreak revenge on Malcolm Turnbull, the scene was set for the tearing down of the prime minister. Home affairs minister Peter Dutton – who had spearheaded the federal government's hyperbole about African gangs in Melbourne – challenged Turnbull for the Liberal leadership, and thus the prime ministership. He spoke about immigration and infrastructure; conservative colleagues spoke about the need to pull out of the Paris climate agreement. The spectre of such a blatant shift to the right, accompanied by anger about the damage done by the conservative camp to both Turnbull and the government, saw a compromise candidate, Scott Morrison, emerge and triumph.

Morrison is, therefore, a person who has been unexpectedly thrust into a position of both power and authority. And we expect him to be a leader – which, as I have argued in this essay, is a very different thing. For most voters, Morrison arrived in the top job as little more than a series of clichés. He had attained the prime ministership because of a rejection of the agenda of others, not because of his own agenda. Newspapers wrote stories in the first few days of his prime ministership about the usual things: sorting out his cabinet; talking to defence chiefs. But the key task – as usual – seemed to be to establish his authenticity. The cliché machine went into overdrive: a mad supporter of the Sharks football team; a prime minister who (unlike Turnbull) did not eat a meat pie with a knife and fork.

*

I have talked a lot in this essay about the space and time leaders need – and, if they are good, can manipulate – to achieve what they wish to achieve. But if there is one space-and-time factor that has helped shape the leadership on offer in the last decade, it is impatience. Both Malcolm Turnbull and Bill Shorten arrived in federal parliament as the most impatient of men. Both felt entitled to be accelerated into positions of seniority. Both had some of the skills necessary to be a national leader: Turnbull, the advocacy skills of the barrister; Shorten, the negotiating and advocacy skills of the union leader. But, as is now the case with Scott Morrison, neither seemed to have a particular view of where they wanted to lead the country, founded in any broad agenda. That stands in stark contrast with leaders of the past, such as Whitlam, Hawke, Keating and Howard. An agenda or "vision" might not be crucial, according to Heifetz, but it does foster a sense of certainty and direction. Turnbull and Shorten arrived, in their determined fashion, in leadership positions still raw and seemingly dismissive of the business of how the parliament, and all that goes with it, works. They had to learn the art of leadership on the job.

Turnbull was a strange amalgam of leader. He engaged in mudslinging and ugly compromise on policies to try to appease the fractious conservative wing of his party, but these were not tasks that he pulled off with any great conviction or aplomb. Where he was more successful was in the space in which he felt more comfortable: trying to work his way through policies with which he was intellectually engaged as a problem-solver. Remaking the schools funding deal known as Gonski – and stealing it from Labor – was one example of this. The deal with the Obama administration on asylum seekers was another (though obviously not sufficient to resolve the offshore detention issue). It is striking these were so often almost solo projects. He went off and worked on them and brought them back as finished products. But in areas where he sought to bring people together to reach a compromise – notably his early outings on tax reform – he was less successful.

The question that will be debated for years to come is the effect of Turnbull's continual concessions to the conservatives, who came for him despite these repeated and detailed compromise proposals – whether he could have, or should have, stared them down. Every time Turnbull made a concession, the conservatives attacked him for being weak, rather than praising him for accepting their position. Asked at his final press conference as prime minister whether he regretted those concessions, given that the conservatives came for him anyway, Turnbull said:

> What I have done always is to try to keep the party together. And that has meant that from time to time I have had to compromise and make concessions. It's something I learnt from my first time as leader that you have to work so hard to keep the show together. That's the bottom line. But, you know, if you look at what we've achieved, it's a very long list. In terms of energy policy and climate policy, I think the truth is that the Coalition finds it very hard to get agreement on anything to do with emissions. I mean, the National Energy Guarantee was or is a vitally piece of economic reform ... But with a one-seat majority in the House, unless you can command all or almost all your votes, you can't get it past. The emissions issues and climate policy issues have the same problem within the Coalition of, you know, bitterly entrenched views that are actually sort of more ideological views than views based, as I say, in engineering and economics. It's a bit like same-sex marriage used to be. Almost, you know, an insoluble problem. We were able to sort that out. That was a significant achievement in my time as prime minister. I think I was the first prime minister to support legalising same-sex marriage but most importantly was able to get it done.

Was the continual accommodation of the right just a failure of leadership or political management by Malcolm Turnbull – as many saw it – or is it no more than the reality of modern Australian politics and some of the factors I have discussed in this essay that now constrain leaders: minority or small majority governments, the rising power of the party room, the breakdown of collective responsibility? This question will now be tested in the Morrison prime ministership, for there is no reason to think any of these factors are going to go away anytime soon.

Bill Shorten, too, has resorted to mudslinging and to personalising the contest with the prime minister he would refer to as "Turnbull" – in a break from the civility of the past, when the opponent was "the prime minister" or at least "Mr Turnbull." But the Opposition leader is at his best when he leads a team advocating well-thought-through policy that represents a real alternative, at real political risk. It is also true that he has been leading a Labor Party that has learnt the cost of internal division. That means the majority of his fights can be external rather than internal.

Politicians these days spend so much time in their speeches and pronouncements trying to speak in the voice of the people. Yet to do this, they must conflate the policies they want to deliver with the things they think voters want or believe. Some of the excruciating language around the Coalition's company tax plan is a good example of this. The trade minister, Steve Ciobo, said in July on Sky News that the reason large companies, including the banks, should get big tax cuts was to help "mum and dad Australians":

> If we can increase the profitability of these businesses, they can do two things: one, provide a higher return to the everyday mums and dads out there who own these businesses in their superannuation, and that provides for their retirement; but the second thing that it does, is it means that these businesses have more money to pay their workers, more money to invest in making their businesses bigger, so this is all a critical driver of economic growth, and economic growth drives jobs, and that's why the Coalition has been successful at creating a record number of new jobs in Australia, and that's why Labor's approach will see less investment, less growth and less money for everyday mum and dads to be able to provide for their retirements in the future.

Our leaders much less often frame a speech in the ways of old: that is, "I am seeking to be your leader. This is what I think we should do. If you don't like it, don't vote for me, but let me try to persuade you of the case."

And of course, they talk about each other. Whenever a politician of either side is in a tight corner in an interview, they will resort to the least persuasive argument of all: "The other side is worse." In doing so, they feed the disillusionment which we saw splinter the vote in Longman. That disillusionment is based on several decades in which the main political story has been political manoeuvring and coups, along with public episodes of MPs and parties spending taxpayers' money, and decisions that are seen to be taken for wholly political reasons (whether or not they actually were).

*

But what about all those other facets of leadership we have been considering? How do our leaders go in mobilising our society to tackle difficult problems? Have our political leaders identified the challenges facing the nation, let alone been prepared to take them on? Have they been able to manage, or manipulate (in a good way), the debate? Have they protected voices of leadership and dissent in the community, or even listened to them?

It is hard to think of a political leader since the time of John Howard and Kevin Rudd who has been able to galvanise the electorate on a really difficult question facing the country, let alone identify and offer to lead the discussion about it. Abbott may have rallied people to his banner of "stop the boats," but it hardly involved persuading, or managing a debate. He simply appealed to white-hot anger and prejudice and offered a simple, brutal solution.

Howard, in his time, argued for a range of policies and, with his cabinet colleagues, prosecuted the case for them, modified where necessary, and listened to critics. I'm thinking of tax policy here. He ultimately fell because he did not do those things on WorkChoices. But he also broke a silent decades-long consensus that kept race and dog-whistling out of Australian politics. Our leaders have failed us in being unwilling, or unable, to put that genie back in the bottle. Echoing Lyndon Johnson's decisions to escalate America's involvement in Vietnam, Howard also asserted a leadership right to drag us into a war, in this case in Iraq.

In Opposition, Rudd identified a range of issues on which the country had got "stuck" and put forward policies to deal with them: from education funding to the NBN, from climate change to federalism. Plenty of airtime has been devoted to the role Rudd's management style may have played in his downfall – and the failure of Labor in government to deliver on many of those reforms. And there was the small matter of the global financial crisis. But for our purposes, Rudd may be an example of the foibles of trying to run too many complex debates at one time, while also being captured by the modern push for permanent campaigning rather than governing.

Julia Gillard first helped us avoid a lot of hard questions by taking over from Rudd and effectively killing off issues that had been raised under his prime ministership, most notably the resources tax. That didn't make the underlying issues go away, of course. And she made little effort to argue the compromise as a solution to the serious policy issue that had been raised by the tax in the first place. She spent most of her prime ministership simply seeking to keep the ship of government afloat in the face of deadly political opposition from Tony Abbott and the internal disruption of Kevin Rudd. Despite those forces, Gillard did launch a range of big initiatives and national debates: the Royal Commission into Institutional Responses to Child Sexual Abuse; the National Disability Insurance Scheme.

There is virtually nothing good to say about Tony Abbott based on the Heifetz leadership model. He was a divisive leader who did not care about being divisive and who remains an utterly destructive force in Australian politics. He did not seek to lead the country through a debate about dealing with complex issues. He certainly did not protect other voices of leadership and dissent. As Opposition leader and prime minister, on issues such as climate change and asylum seekers, he bastardised the debate to capitalise on the political fallout and left such a mess for his successors that it was almost impossible for the country to have a rational discussion about them.

To be a leader, you don't necessarily have to have a vision, but you either have to know what it is that you want to persuade other people to do, or else have the knack of identifying and synthesising an issue on which people are seeking leadership. You also need to know how you are going to do something about such issues. And you have to know which are the most important things to get done at any given point in time. Then you have to make the rest of us understand why these things are important and what you are going to do about them. This task might simply be an echo of a crystallised or uncrystallised public mood. Or something that involves reimagining all the barriers and structures around a difficult issue.

But it does ultimately require you to bring people with you. And this was something Abbott failed to do, just as he failed to identify the most important things to be done. His government collapsed under the weight of pushing hard policies like those of the 2014 Budget without being able to persuade voters. And it floundered in the mud of unimportant, sometimes ludicrous, controversies, like a knighthood for the husband of the Queen and protecting the rights of racists.

The other thing you need to do as a leader is decide whether you are going to engage in transactional or transformative change. Malcolm Turnbull did not promise transformation; nor does Bill Shorten. Scott Morrison's capacity to do so is constrained by the circumstances in which he has risen to the prime ministership: only months to a general election; having to fight a by-election and possibly lose majority government; the difficulties involved in reorienting a government with personnel changes and new messages.

In Turnbull's case, his capacity to be transformational was constrained by that initial impatience: he inherited a raft of policies laid down by his predecessor, Abbott, and had to spend the first couple of years of his prime ministership tactfully unwinding them. (There was an expectation he could simply do away with all the difficulties.) He was also constrained by his own history: his previous unhappy stint as leader of his party left him having to double down on efforts to look consultative and thus unable to assert an agenda of his own for the government.

Bill Shorten has not had that problem. But he is also constrained by his own history: his role in bringing down two prime ministers, which puts him at the centre of the story of politicians mostly focused on political manoeuvrings rather than national leadership. He wears the constraint of disappointed expectations felt by the electorate in the aftermath of the Rudd project, and by the sense of incompetence and infighting left in the minds of many Australians by Labor's revolving door of leadership between 2010 and 2013 – itself a product of impatience.

In September 2018, Malcolm Turnbull was due to become the longest-serving Australian prime minister since John Howard, having survived in the job for three years – the normal first term of a prime minister, a period in which they are just getting started on the agenda for which they argued from Opposition. Reaching that milestone may have helped the country – or at least the political class – reset its expectations of politics and political leadership. It may have started the long process of changing the discussion of our country's woes from narrow critiques of leaders' personal strengths and weaknesses to more grown-up consideration of the complexities of the issues we face, and indeed the difficulties and compromises our political leaders confront in finding solutions to them. Instead, the Liberal Party has been ripped apart and even further divided, it faces political defeat at the next election, and our polity is worse off for having one of its major political parties rendered largely ungovernable.

Measured against Ronald Heifetz's definition of leadership, how do we judge Malcolm Turnbull and Bill Shorten? Heifetz defined leadership as helping a community embrace change, offering a map, a clear option to deal with a problem, and corralling factions to a compromise. For him, leadership is about possessing the skills with which to read and push a community.

Bill Shorten's greatest Heifetz moment on leadership remains the National Disability Insurance Scheme. He, more than anyone, was responsible for this. Given the disability portfolio when he came into parliament in 2007, Shorten set out to find a goal that would unite a notoriously fractured sector, and he stubbornly pushed it onto the agenda, often against considerable resistance from senior ministers.

Since becoming leader, Shorten has been prepared to do many of the things that Heifetz would define as true leadership. He and his colleagues went to the 2016 election offering policies on tax – including negative gearing – that for decades had been regarded as political poison. The most important thing was not that it was a brave thing to do, but that Labor had a plan and argued persistently, calmly and rationally for it. Labor didn't rely on simply attacking the other side. It offered voters an alternative – to accept or reject – on a range of important issues, including housing, Indigenous affairs and the republic.

Bill Shorten offers the best test of the countervailing pressures on and perceptions of our political leaders. Published polling and focus groups repeatedly report that voters just don't like Shorten. Yet he has set out a path. We don't know how he would perform as a prime ministerial consensus-builder.

In what were to prove the last days of the Turnbull era, Labor hedged its bets on the politically difficult issue of energy and climate policy. Labor was quietly hoping the Coalition would succeed in introducing the National Energy Guarantee – the barest of frameworks, but a framework nonetheless, for energy and climate after a decade of policy destruction. But Turnbull was left out in no-man's-land to fight all the forces arrayed against him, with Labor unwilling to leave the trenches and offer any signs of early bipartisanship to get the deal through. And it says much about the state of internal politics in the Coalition that the prime minister believed he could not do the obvious thing and use Labor support for the policy to overcome his own shortage of numbers to get the legislation through the parliament. Too many people in the Coalition would have seen such bipartisanship as completely unacceptable.

Conceived by the people appointed to give government the best available advice on energy policy, the National Energy Guarantee neatly bundled up the need to reduce emissions with the more recent crisis over energy supply and prices. Yet its design also highlighted that our politicians don't feel brave enough to talk about climate change anymore. It has become an addendum. Malcolm Turnbull said the policy would allow the energy sector to meet Australia's international commitments, knowing that this sector alone could not offset growing emissions elsewhere. The difficulty of securing agreement from the states reflected how complex so much policy has become in recent years. But it was striking that "stakeholders" from green groups and business alike were back in play to encourage our politicians to make the right decision.

Turnbull's National Energy Guarantee represented an attempt to give us a clear path through a difficult issue, to bring parties together to a compromise and consensus. It offered an end to a national stalemate and the prospect of a policy that could get better in the future. Importantly, it would have been a victory for leadership by many in the community, a sign that we are still capable of having many different voices heard on an important matter. Yet the greatest difficulty the prime minister, and therefore the government, faced was an internal one. From the bloody-minded and vengeful determination of Tony Abbott to destroy Turnbull's authority, to the coal warriors, to those who simply wanted firmer action on energy prices, the Coalition's collective death wish made resolution of the policy impossible. All sides were going to have to make concessions to get a suite of workable policies agreed upon. But instead of engaging in clear-eyed internal discussion about what options were open to it, the Coalition plunged into a confused orgy of opportunism. Turnbull, as the deal-maker, was attacked when he did not propose concessions, and then savagely attacked when he did.

The instability that grew around Malcolm Turnbull's prime ministership only confirms the extent to which we see political developments through the lens of their impact on leaders. Maybe it is always partially true that the personal drives the broader drama. But the suggestion that all actions are driven by a leader's selfish need for self-preservation has also become a lethal weapon in the hands of political opponents. Turnbull's moves to find a consensus between the polarised positions, not just in his party but also with the states and the Opposition, were portrayed relentlessly by the News Corp papers as both weak and designed solely to shore up his leadership. The idea that changes actually addressed criticisms that had been made of the policy disappeared into the mist.

Malcolm Turnbull's downfall, and the fate of his prime ministership more broadly, came down to a series of judgments made not just by him, but by his colleagues, who, having elevated him as their best prospect of retaining power in 2016, spent much of his prime ministership failing to follow the leader and also failing in their own collective responsibility for leadership.

*

Australia today faces a range of complex, politically difficult issues, which go to our identity and the nature of our society. There are pressing international dilemmas, too. Yet issues such as Indigenous recognition, population and climate change have either been pushed off the table, buried in other issues where we might not notice them, or risk becoming ugly and dangerous debates which divide people rather than bring them together.

A large part of the job of political leadership now, which goes completely unrecognised, is rebuilding the national political discussion after years of it being under assault. Maybe that will only happen if and when our political leaders recognise that their own room to move is going to be vastly expanded if there are other leaders in the community with whom they can speak. In Heifetz's terms, our leaders are doing little to protect "voices of leadership in the community," voices whose standing has been diminished by the collapse of many of the institutions they once represented, and who are therefore too easily relegated to the lesser standing of stakeholder, with all its connotations of compromised self-interest. A great start would be to end the practice of shooting the messenger – whether it be the Human Rights Commission or others who are simply doing what they have been asked to do – and to restore the practice of inviting in community groups to discuss an issue, rather than merely going through the motions of doing so.

In a climate where so many of the historic sources of authority and power in our society have been diminished, the pressure is on our political leaders to take up the issues that rumble along beneath the surface but which seem too hard to touch; to confront our community with them and to help us find a way through.

So many of them have not just been shoved in a cupboard as too hard, but delegitimised by politics itself. We are not quite sure yet how we will tackle not just the complexities of our relationships with China and the United States, but what we will do about the collapsing international consensus, and our leaders have not given us a map. Our position on human rights at home and abroad has been whittled away little by little in the name of national security and tighter borders, and in the name of dog-whistling racism. We choose not to look or comprehend. And eventually we forget what we used to believe in as a country on these issues.

Income inequality requires a clear redefinition or restatement of the social contract governments have with individuals. We must contemplate the impact of immigration on our population and the capacity of the country to continue to absorb more people, instead of bumbling on refusing to talk about it but failing to build the infrastructure – of all descriptions – that high immigration levels have always required.

To do this, our political leaders will have to counter, rather than encourage or be sustained by, the profound stupidity of the culture wars. But they must also be able to coax those who are encouraged or reinforced by them back into the realm of intelligent debate devoid of false divisions.

In this, there is a responsibility for those in the media – which does so much to set the terms of public debate – to think often and hard about what we cover, and how we cover it. Unfortunately, we live in an era where, despite the collapse of traditional media, the remaining moguls are prepared to throw their weight around, building up and tearing down leaders, seemingly at will. It is so often the media that set up a straw-man call for "strong" leaders, appearing not to contemplate where that might lead us, despite the horror show that is now the US presidency. In reviewing for this essay developments in the US and the UK, and in Germany and France, it has been striking how different the public debates are in countries where Rupert Murdoch and his media outlets do not have a presence.

The biggest issue for our leaders, however, may be how we respond to the rise of autocracies and strongman politics around the world and the decline of democracy and multilateralism. The world is becoming more irrational, and we cannot assume that other nations will even pretend to seek mutually beneficial relationships. If we still believe in the ways of democracy and pluralism, our leaders should be practising these things at home, as well as advocating their continuation abroad.

*

For political leaders who do not defy convention in the spectacular fashion of Donald Trump, the greatest challenge is often not to determine where the country is going, but to persuade first their colleagues and then the voters where they should go.

Doris Kearns Goodwin's book *Team of Rivals* documents Abraham Lincoln's genius around the cabinet table. Lincoln's political genius lay in the fact that he was not just willing to bring his rivals for the Republican Party's presidential nomination into his cabinet, but actively pursued them, even though many were contemptuous of the backwoods lawyer and in shock that he had come through the middle of the field to beat them all. It is the story of how they came to respect and follow him.

Our view of leadership in Australia has become sadly one-dimensional. To see how leaders around the world are dealing with complexity should cause us to consider our politicians differently. We should always have great expectations of them, but we need to judge them on more than their performance in the polls or their authenticity. We must accept the need for pragmatism and compromise – after all, minority government is the outcome of the way we voted, not something imposed on us by politicians.

Australia's splintered politics limit the room for bold gestures and ideas. Even so, such ideas are out there, and should be seized. But we need our leaders to be wary of simple solutions built on scapegoating and hatred, and to resist succumbing to those who relentlessly conjure up reasons for intolerance. We should expect our leaders to help rebuild the national debate and protect other voices within it. We should be looking for strong leaders to follow, not a strongman.

27 August 2018

ACKNOWLEDGMENTS AND SOURCES

This has been the most difficult of my three Quarterly Essays to write, given both the complex nature of the subject and the rapidly morphing state of political leadership. Among those I can thank publicly for their contributions are Elouise Fowler, Jacob Greber, Paul Ham, Travers McLeod, Rory Medcalf, Jim Middleton, Michael Neill, Martin Stuart-Weekes and Hugh White. More than ever, Chris Feik has been not just a superb editor but a great source of ideas.

For Sam Neill, Global Leader (Top Bloke Division)
"What a funny business."

6–7 "Liberal democracies": Francis Fukuyama, "How to Tame the Populists", in *The Future of Politics*, Credit Suisse Research Institute, published to coincide with the World Economic Forum at Davos, January 2018.

17 "to focus on": "Britain Has Had Enough of Experts, says Gove", *The Financial Times*, 4 June 2016.

20 "You cannot know": "Thinking the Unthinkable: A new imperative for leadership in the digital age. An interim report by Nik Gowing and Chris Langdon", Public Purpose, June 2018.

20–1 "Part of the challenge": "President Obama and Marilynne Robinson: A Conversation—II", *The New York Review of Books*, 19 November 2015.

22 "One of the interesting things": Obama dinner, Auckland, March 2018.

25–6 "the health, mental stability," etc.: John Lewis Gaddis, *On Grand Strategy*, Penguin Random House, UK, 2018.

26 "Germany's newly minted leader", etc.: Paul Ham, *Young Hitler: The Making of the Führer*, Penguin Random House, Australia, 2017.

29 "intended to mobilize", etc.: Ronald A. Heifetz, *Leadership Without Easy Answers*, Harvard University Press, 1994.

33 "that moment in most presidencies", etc.: Jeff Shesol, "Obama and the End of Greatness", *The New Yorker*, 22 October 2014.

35–6 "the dreamer and the realist": David Runciman, "The Impermanence of Importance", *London Review of Books*, vol. 40, no. 15, 2 August 2018.

36 "One of the many things": Miranda Carter, "What Happens When a Bad-Tempered, Distractable Doofus Runs an Empire?" *The New Yorker*, 6 June 2018.

44 "She knew that diving", etc.: Matthew Qvortrup, *Angela Merkel: Europe's most influential leader*, Duckworth Overlook, 2016.

51 "Today, French citizens": Emmanuel Macron, *Revolution*, translated by Jonathan Goldberg and Juliette Scott, Scribe, 2017.

52 "devotion to the charisma": Max Weber's "Politics as a Vocation" originated in the second lecture of a series he gave in Munich to the "Free Students Union" of Bavaria on 28 January 1919. http://www.generation-online.org/p/fpweber.htm.

71–2 "democratisation of foreign policy", etc.: "Can Democracy Deliver?" John Menadue Oration by Marty Natalegawa, Melbourne, 2 November 2017.

DEAD RIGHT

Correspondence

John McTernan

Now, I am no defender of neoliberalism – the precise opposite – but judging from this essay, neoliberalism is under no threat.

Early in my career as an adviser, I was writing a speech for my boss. I ran an early draft past an older hand, who told me: "Whenever you get to a weak point in your argument, you attack Margaret Thatcher or the Tories. Cut out the attacks and strengthen your argument!" That advice has rung in my ears ever since when drafting polemic texts. It is a profound shame that apparently no one has ever taken Richard Denniss aside and given him similar advice. I am sure that somewhere in this rant that masquerades as an essay there is an argument, but you would be hard pressed to find it. Instead, the words "neoliberal" and "neoliberalism" are used incontinently – over one hundred times, nearly twice a page.

Of course, this is an essay on "how neoliberalism ate itself," so one expects the word to be used. But there is a gap at the centre of Denniss's argument: he fails to define his terms. He wants to slay a dragon, but to defeat an argument you need to articulate it, and in this essay you search and search for a credible definition of "neoliberalism" in vain. It flickers in and out of sight, always in the distance and on the horizon, but – to paraphrase Gertrude Stein – when you think you've got there, "there's no there there."

It would be tedious to give all of the competing and conflicting definitions of "neoliberalism" that Denniss uses, but here's a short list. Neoliberalism is:

- small government
- sponsorship of museums
- looking out for yourself
- the last thirty years of Australian government
- outsourcing public services
- cultural change of hearts and minds
- the profit motive

- measuring efficiency and quality
- the assertion "there is no alternative"
- reducing the budget deficit and public spending
- cutting regulation
- the idea that market forces are superior to government decision-making.

I could go on, and indeed Denniss does, but unlike him I care too much for the reader.

Simply put, neoliberalism is whatever he dislikes, not just from time to time but from paragraph to paragraph. The saddest thing is that he knows that this is a candidate for the Miles Franklin Award rather than a serious piece of political commentary, writing at one point: "the policy agenda of neoliberalism has never been broadly applied in Australia." Showstopper, much?

Perhaps you think I'm being unfair. Let me quote some key extracts. Unlike many miserabilists, he does offer a potential solution, but it is as opaque as it is vague: "So, what is to be done? Embrace populism."

Populism, you won't be surprised, goes undefined.

Denniss does, though, promote a reform agenda. Quixotically, he argues for more pollies: "While neoliberalism has trained us to think we already waste too much money on politicians, the fact is we have not nearly enough of them for them to do their jobs well."

And his radical policy agenda? Front and centre is euthanasia:

> The overwhelming majority of Australians support voluntary euthanasia. But as with equal marriage, historical and cultural legacies in the major parliamentary parties mean that passing laws that give people suffering chronic pain a degree of choice (a very neoliberal benefit) is currently beyond most of our parliaments. A free vote or plebiscite on such an issue would almost certainly lead to significant change that would appeal both to libertarians and to most people concerned with social justice.

As the senior bureaucrat says in *Yes, Prime Minister*, "Bold." This is far from the most urgent of the challenges facing Australia in the twenty-first century, as even Denniss agrees, judging from the pressing problems he lists in his essay.

What is the fundamental problem of this essay? The clue is evident throughout in the constant reference to impersonal authority:

- "neoliberalism has succeeded"
- "neoliberalism has trained us"

- "neoliberalism has made us more selfish"
- "if neoliberalism has taught us anything"
- "[neoliberalism] laid claim to words like 'efficiency,' 'productivity' and 'growth'".

This is remarkable. Everything is done to Australia, but no one is doing it. In the language of the playground, "A big boy did it and he ran away."

This is the fundamental problem. Politics, in the end, is about choices and the allocation of resources – across ages, genders, regions and so on. Politics is about agency – and Denniss denies that to anyone in Australia. Things just happen – like the weather in Britain. Worse, his comically inept inability to define neoliberalism means that he allows a genuinely destructive mode of politics and economics to escape criticism. At one stage, Denniss seems to believe that neoliberalism can be defined as caring about value for money. On the one hand, for anyone who has ever had to balance a bank account, that is laughable. On the other, it is a massive concession – if that's what he thinks neoliberalism is, then it makes sense to almost everyone. Hands up who wants government to waste money? In fighting shadows, Denniss legitimises what he opposes.

As he writes at one point, "Words matter." And, as Freud would have recognised, Denniss's own words are the most revealing:

> The political right is hoist with its own petard. They were willing to destroy much of the public's faith in experts and institutions to protect their friends in the fossil-fuel industry from what were, in theory, neoliberal policy tools such as the carbon tax and the mining tax.

The carbon tax and the mining tax are, of course, not neoliberal – they are simply market mechanisms. Here's the rub: Denniss's essay is not about neoliberalism at all. It's about conservatism as an ideology – and its failure in Australia. Properly written, it would be a fascinating piece. But, for some reason, he feels the need to assert that Hawke, Keating, Howard, Rudd and Gillard – five very different prime ministers, four of them Labor – all governed according to a single neoliberal ideology. He is, to coin a phrase, Dead Wrong.

John McTernan

W. Max Corden

Right at the beginning of this essay we are told that neoliberalism is "the catch-all term for all things small government." Later, on page 18, we are told convincingly that "Australian politics isn't about ideology, it is about interests." I assume from the context that "neoliberalism" is the ideology the author is writing about. Since neoliberalism has numerous definitions and interpretations in the world (notably in Latin America), it is thus best to ignore this confusing, ghastly term and get down to business. What really matters in Australia and other countries are "interests." Possibly there is no relevant ideology governing our rulers other than self-interest (of individuals, groups and companies).

The author is concerned with the harmful influence and language of our political and business right-wing advocates and commentators. Call them the "elite." Possibly this language masquerades as ideology and obscures the importance of their "interests." There are two issues he discusses. I think both are extremely important.

The first concerns the size of government and (in the views of the elite) the need to keep this size as low as possible, for whatever reason. It is a right-wing obsession. This also involves the desirability of shifting many activities from government to privatisation. If one judges episodes of privatisation by the actual effects on costs and quality of services received by consumers, we have important examples in Australia of extreme failure. The author refers to these, and it seems to me that more detailed and comprehensive analysis of such private-sector failures is needed. But the evidence so far is remarkable. Well-known cases in Australia are the privatisation of national electricity supply and the privatisation of vocational training and education. What has gone wrong in these cases and why do measures that foster competition among private providers often fail?

Most recently, right-wing elements of the Liberal Party have apparently proposed that there is no "economic" justification for the Australian Broadcasting

Commission (ABC). This seems to imply that it should be privatised (or even abolished). This is likely to be widely discussed, so it just comes under this general category of reducing the size of government. Australia's right-wingers seem to have an obsession in this area. Are government agencies really so bad? And who would gain from ABC privatisation? In this case, as others, there is a notable use or possibly misuse of the term "economic."

The second big issue has to do with the national budget. As Denniss writes, "reducing the budget deficit is very, very important." It is what "neoliberals really seem to believe." He notes that whenever some social spending (that he approves of) is proposed, the so-called neoliberals (meaning the right-wing elite) oppose it for the sake of avoiding or reducing a budget deficit. But then, he points out (and elaborates), they find many ways of spending for purposes they approve of, while opposing expenditures for social purposes.

There is no doubt that this essay by Denniss conveys an impression of bias on the part of its author, but as a reader of Murdoch's *The Australian* I am inured to that from the other side. The author covers many interesting issues: for example, the difficulties of devising adequate rules and regulations to protect consumers in a "free" market, and why some monopolies are inevitable.

An ambitious final chapter, "Government Is Good," is well worth thinking about, though, admittedly, I am somewhat sceptical. In this chapter, Denniss is full of ideas. He thinks there is too much emphasis on increasing the rate of growth, and especially that there is a tendency to blame the unemployed for their unemployment. He wants to see re-established a broad debate about the national interest. Strikingly and convincingly, he argues that the right-wing war on government and tax is, in reality, a war on democracy. He wants to see a revitalisation of faith in democracy, and he thinks there is a need for an improvement in the popular education of democratic processes. And, in addition to all that, he wants a whole lot of new institutions: a charter of rights, a national interest commission (to guide on what is good for the country), a federal corruption watchdog, a sovereign wealth fund, and – surprise, surprise – an end of talk about the economy all the time. The following sums up his ambitious message: "For thirty years our elected leaders have endlessly debated what is good for business or good for the economy, but it is time that we commenced a broader debate about what is good for the nation."

He seems to be somewhat uncomfortable with the Productivity Commission, though some of his proposals go close to expanding the Commission's activities. One of his ambitious suggestions for comprehensive reviews comes close to the Commission's comprehensive "Shifting the Dial" review.

With some reservations, I would certainly recommend Denniss's essay, especially the last chapter, to anyone (especially politicians) who wants to sponsor non-economic but radical social and administrative reforms in Australia.

W. Max Corden

John Quiggin

As Richard Denniss observes, the ideology of neoliberalism – or, in common Australian parlance, "economic rationalism" – a set of ideas so dominant as to seem like common sense, at least to the political class, has, quite suddenly, lost its grip on thinking about public policy.

The political right in Australia now routinely advocates government intervention to achieve all kinds of goals, from the preservation of coal-fired electricity generation to the construction of sporting stadiums. The Labor Party, which took the lead in the early years of neoliberal reform, has shifted even further, advocating higher taxes on companies and high-income taxpayers to fund measures like the NDIS and Gonski programs.

On the other hand, as Denniss notes, neoliberalism (like every other ideology in history) has never been applied in its purest forms. Cosy deals with favoured businesses on the one hand and occasional gestures towards social equity on the other can be observed through the 1980s, 1990s and 2000s. What, if anything, is different today?

Before starting, it's important to distinguish between "hard" neoliberalism and the "soft" neoliberalism sometimes called the "Third Way." Hard neoliberalism, most prominently represented by Margaret Thatcher, combined market-oriented policies of privatisation and pro-business regulation with attacks on social welfare and regressive income redistribution. Its high point in Australia was the Fightback! package put forward by John Hewson in 1993. Following the unexpected defeat of Fightback!, John Howard and Peter Costello pursued a more cautious version of the same agenda.

In contrast, soft neoliberalism involved an attempt to soften the impact of neoliberal policies by strengthening the welfare "safety net" and maintaining some progressivity in the tax system. The successive versions of the Accord under the Hawke government were the most notable embodiment of soft neoliberalism in Australia. Within the Hawke government, there was a sustained tension between the soft neoliberalism of the Accord and the hard neoliberalism of Paul Keating and Peter Walsh.

From the 1980s to the global financial crisis, the range of opinion from "hard" to "soft" neoliberalism defined the Overton Window, representing the range of opinions that could be taken seriously within the Australian political class. As Laura Tingle observed as recently as 2015, in her Quarterly Essay *Political Amnesia*, to argue against economic rationalism was to invite "ridicule or contempt." In retrospect, the fact that such arguments were even deemed worthy of mention was an indicator that the grip of economic rationalism was loosening.

In both its hard and soft forms, neoliberalism was an elite project relying on a broad consensus within the political class. Neoliberalism never attracted strong public support; rather, it relied on acquiescence and acceptance of Thatcher's dictum that "there is no alternative," acronymically abbreviated as TINA.

But in the wake of the global financial crisis, even that acquiescence disappeared. For a political class still saturated in neoliberal ideas, this represented a crisis of legitimacy. The public was no longer listening to talk about markets and choice, but the political class was still in thrall to these ideas. Again, Laura Tingle captured the problem (from the perspective of the political class) in her 2012 Quarterly Essay, *Great Expectations*.

The breakdown of neoliberalism, in Australia and throughout the English-speaking world, has been most dramatic on the political right. In the absence of mass enthusiasm for neoliberalism, the right has long relied for electoral support on a combination of class support from big and small business, hostility towards trade unions, and appeals to social attitudes which could, until recently, be described as "conservative," including attachment to the monarchy, traditional family values and faith in strong leaders. Where necessary, these were backed up by appeals to racial and religious bigotry, sometimes overt, but mostly coded as opposition to "political correctness."

Taken together, one might call this "default identity politics." It's the inverse image of what's commonly referred to as "identity politics," based on membership of a minority or (in the case of gender) underrepresented group. The default identity is one that is taken to be typical of people in the country concerned, and entitled to deference from others who differ in various ways from the default.

The core claim of default identity politics is that these "real Australians" (or "real Americans," etc. have been ignored and overridden by a minority who do not share their values – radicals, foreigners, elites and so on. Although this theme is an old one, going back to Robert Menzies' "forgotten people," it has gained in intensity as the population has become more diverse, with the result that only a minority of people fit the default identity.

The result has been a proliferation of minor parties, of the far right, right and centre right. Examples in the last two Senates include Pauline Hanson's One Nation; Australian Conservatives; the Palmer United Party, aka the United Australia Party; Family First; Katter's Australian Party; and Derryn Hinch's Justice Party. Some of these parties represent specific components of the right-wing base, some are personal vehicles for aspiring demagogues and some a mixture of the two.

Although not a major source of electoral support, the coherent policy direction of neoliberalism provided the glue that held this coalition together. The collapse of faith in neoliberalism has dissolved the glue.

Abbott's term as leader of the Opposition and then as prime minister completed the eclipse of neoliberalism. Consider his three-word slogans: "Axe the Tax," "Stop the Boats" and "Fix the Debt." Axe the Tax represented Abbott's rejection of a market-based response to climate change. Stop the Boats was a gesture to the prejudices of the base. Fix the Debt was code for the neoliberal program embodied in the Commission of Audit report and Joe Hockey's 2014 Budget. But the message was too deeply hidden for the voters to understand that Abbott's promises to protect public expenditure were (in the terminology made famous by John Howard) "non-core." Once the 2014 Budget failed, concerns about neoliberal orthodoxy were finished.

In particular, concerns about the "level playing field" disappeared. Industries were supported or punished according to their position in Abbott's culture war politics. The vehicle industry was punished because the companies were seen as being in league with the unions. Coal was promoted, while solar energy was denounced. Even more absurdly, bogus claims about the health risks of sound from wind turbines were promoted by the very same people who had spent decades deriding environmental concerns of all kinds.

Abbott's replacement by Malcolm Turnbull seemed to promise the possibility of a shift to soft neoliberalism. Turnbull had mouthed all the right words during his previous stint as leader and throughout his period in the wilderness. As prime minister, however, he turned out to stand for nothing except handouts to his own class. He embraced, or acquiesced in, climate-science denialism, culture wars on marriage and refugees, and, finally, outright racism.

The change is evident in a comparison with the first upsurge of One Nation in the late 1990s. At that time, the mainstream conservative parties had enough self-confidence to reject Hanson. Strikingly, Tony Abbott led a legal vendetta against Hanson, which led to her being jailed for supposed violations of electoral law (the charges were, quite properly, overturned on appeal).

By contrast, the second time around, the LNP was eager to find that Hanson had "matured." In reality, Hanson's racism and bigotry were more entrenched than ever, but were now in tune with those of the dominant groups in the LNP base, led, ironically, by Tony Abbott.

On the left, the picture during the era of neoliberalism was a mirror image of that on the right. Under Hawke and Keating, Labor led the way in promoting a soft version of neoliberalism. Environmentalists, feminists and old-fashioned Labor voters might have been disillusioned by the politics of privatisation and deregulation but they had nowhere else to go. Labor lost support to the Greens but got most of it back in second preferences.

In the wake of the global financial crisis, the contradictions emerged in full force. After Kevin Rudd's brief flirtation with a reinvigorated social democracy in his *Monthly* essay on the crisis, Labor retreated to the familiar ground of soft neoliberalism for the remainder of its time in office.

Yet in the last few years, the spell of neoliberalism has faded. Labor has proposed higher taxes and increased public expenditure, and has largely, though not entirely, repudiated privatisation and asset sales. There hasn't been any obvious electoral cost to this; rather, Labor has been consistently ahead in Newspolls federally and has gained ground at the state level.

This process has been far from painless. There have also been some curious realignments. Bill Shorten, long seen as a right-wing opportunist, has taken a series of stands bolder than anything seen from Labor in decades. Meanwhile, Anthony Albanese, long the darling of the party's progressive membership, has attacked Shorten from the right, calling for pro-business economic policies and surrender to Turnbull's class war. Overall, however, the shift away from soft neoliberalism is unmistakable.

Why has the realignment gone more smoothly on the left than on the right? In part, the breakdown on the right has assisted the process of change on the left. The collapse of hard neoliberalism has undermined the capacity of the right to make any coherent argument on economic policy. It's obvious, for example, from the Turnbull government's flailing around on tax policy that the cuts it eventually introduced were driven by class interest rather than by any real faith in markets.

In part, it's a matter of generational turnover, as leaders whose political views were formed in the economic upheaval of the 1970s and 1980s pass from the scene. These leaders were saturated in neoliberal ideology and took as obvious common sense the worship of financial markets central to that ideology. Younger activists, who have experienced the chaos and corruption of weakly regulated financial markets, find laughable the idea that the fluctuations of these markets represent the considered judgment of experts.

It is important not to be complacent about this. Bad as hard neoliberalism was, its collapse has opened the way for the darker and more dangerous forces of racism and bigotry, which now dominate the political right in Australia, and around the world. In the long run, these forces will be defeated, as they always have been. But the damage that can be done in the meantime is huge.

It is clear, however, that a policy of cautious compromise is not going to work. The only alternative to the right-wing politics of fear is a left-wing politics of hope.

John Quiggin

DEAD RIGHT

Correspondence

Kristina Keneally

"Remind me again how socialism causes lines," I texted to my husband as I stood in a forty-minute queue in a car rental agency at Denver International Airport a few weeks ago. He was sitting on a bench outside the building, in the sunshine, minding our luggage. He definitely had the better end of the deal.

There we were, in the supposed home of laissez-faire capitalism, waiting in a long line for a car we had prebooked, because the big car rental company we were patronising had no reason to improve its customer service. The car rental industry in America is overregulated and dominated by a handful of companies. These companies know that customers have to cop long waits. Market rules and regulations don't allow innovative competitors to emerge that might provide customers with a more efficient service.

Richard Denniss's essay *Dead Right* provides similar examples of how private businesses in Australia rely on market rules, often set by right-wing governments, that protect their market share and increase their profits at the expense of consumers.

This is not very neoliberal.

In the past few years, a great deal has been written critiquing neoliberalism and pronouncing it dead. The rise of protectionism and the rejection of global free trade in countries like the United States and Britain is meant to prove that neoliberalism is a failed project.

Denniss's essay doesn't exactly traverse this path. His aim is not to demonstrate that neoliberalism itself has failed, but rather to show that the right wing of politics has killed it off. The wider community no longer believes neoliberal claims, Denniss argues, because people can see that the political right has been using neoliberal arguments to run down public institutions while giving market advantage and public money to their friends in big business.

Consider the Coalition government's recent announcement of $444 million, described by the former prime minister as "the single biggest contribution and investment in the Great Barrier Reef ever." The purpose of the funding is to help arrest recent environmental damage to the Great Barrier Reef and safeguard this significant natural asset into the future.

However, the government bypassed the public agencies with direct responsibility for the Reef, like the CSIRO and the Great Barrier Reef Marine Park Authority, and instead awarded all 444 million taxpayer dollars to a private organisation, the Great Barrier Reef Foundation.

The Great Barrier Reef Foundation is a creature of the private sector. It is backed by big mining companies like BHP and Rio Tinto, energy companies like AGL, ConocoPhillips and Peabody Energy, three of the big four banks, and industry bodies like the Business Council of Australia.

The Coalition government undertook no advertised grant application or tender process for this funding. According to evidence given to Senate hearings, the government didn't consult with either the Authority, the CSIRO or the Foundation's board until after it decided to give the Foundation the money. The CEO of the Foundation, Anna Marsden, described the grant, which is fifty-five times its 2016 budget, as "like we've just won lotto."

The government says the reason it directed the funds to the Foundation rather than the Authority is because the Foundation will be able to "leverage" additional money from other businesses for the reef. Yet there is little evidence the Foundation has the capacity to do so, and no indication how much money that leverage could generate for the reef.

With this one announcement, the government has placed the future of a World Heritage site in private hands, and a huge wad of public money in the Foundation's bank account.

The Great Barrier Reef Foundation has six full-time employees. When questioned at Senate estimates as to how the government could have confidence that a small organisation could manage such a large grant of government funds and implement the necessary environmental protection programs on behalf of taxpayers, a Department of the Environment official, Stephen Oxley, said:

> We had a look at the overall composition of the board … there is a long list of people who have extensive experience in the corporate and philanthropic and research science sectors who collectively are, I think, very well-regarded Australians, and I think we can be reasonably confident in their capacity to oversee the operations of the foundation.

A few weeks later, the ACCC charged Great Barrier Reef Foundation board director Stephen Roberts with criminal cartel offences related to his time as country head at Citigroup. By the next day, Mr Roberts had stepped down from the Foundation's board and his name and picture were removed from its website.

A Senate inquiry into the Great Barrier Reef Foundation grant is now underway. What should have been a positive announcement for the Reef is turning into a headache for the Coalition government, and another big blow to neoliberalism's reputation.

Denniss considers what we should do in the wake of neoliberalism's demise. I hope that the death of neoliberalism might lead to a more vibrant, creative, imaginative political discussion. Neoliberalism relies on fear to narrow our political debate to suit its terms: the range of policy options is artificially limited by dire warnings of lost credit ratings, debt and deficit emergencies, and lost competitiveness. These things are important, but they should not be considered in isolation, or over and above other options that could be on the table.

For example, the right wing of politics is constantly pointing to the United States, claiming we need to cut our company tax rate because that country has done so. Why don't we ever seriously debate other examples? Scandinavian countries make different choices to the US when it comes to corporate and personal tax rates and social services spending, and their nations have some of the happiest populations on earth. Surely our political debate can consider a wider range of options than the neoliberal prescription.

The fact that Labor has been able to take on one of the "sacred cows" of Australian politics by proposing to curtail negative gearing without igniting a massive scare campaign suggests that the political dynamic in our country is changing – I say for the better.

Still, there are risks ahead for Australian democracy and political debate. The Business Council of Australia isn't taking the death of neoliberalism lying down: instead, the BCA seeks to reincarnate neoliberalism in a more community-friendly guise. It recently set up an innocuous-sounding community organisation called Centre Ground as a front group. Centre Ground is wholly owned by the BCA, and Andrew Bragg, a former Liberal Party executive director and current BCA executive director for members, is one of Centre Ground's directors.

Centre Ground's main activity is to run a phoney grassroots campaign called "For the Common Good." Designed to look and sound like a real community campaign (a tactic known as "astroturfing"), For the Common Good supports pro-business policies. The Common Good campaign pushed for a change to South Australian trading hours in that state's recent elections. The BCA didn't acknowledge its sponsorship of the Common Good campaign in South Australia until ten days after the polls closed. Similarly, voters in the recent Tasmanian and Queensland by-elections who saw Common Good advertising would not have been easily able to identify that the BCA was behind these efforts.

A healthy democracy requires transparency. Such attempts by political actors like the BCA to obscure their sponsorship and motivations should concern us.

While Denniss does not mention the BCA's astroturfing efforts, he does dwell on the need to bolster our democratic system and safeguard it from veiled interference, especially online. He argues that we ought to focus on strengthening our democracy to empower the many over vested interests.

I think this is right. I agree with Denniss that we can never take for granted that the particular characteristics of Australian democracy – such as compulsory voting and compulsory preferential voting – are permanent and enduring. It is fundamental that our citizens understand and value these strengths.

I would add to Denniss's list the independent Australian Electoral Commission, which allows us to avoid the partisan gerrymandering that occurs in the United States. Our democracy would be further strengthened with more timely transparency, if not immediate disclosure, of political donations. Federally, we should also consider caps on political expenditure and donations, as some Australian states have done. And, of course, we should implement a ban on foreign donations.

I wholeheartedly endorse Denniss's call for a national federal corruption body. In February 2018, Labor announced that in government we will create the National Integrity Commission.

I also agree with Denniss that plebiscites may well be a way to revive Australians' interest and trust in political decisions. In the wake of the Irish vote in the same-sex marriage referendum, I proposed that a plebiscite might be a way through the Australian federal parliament's impasse on marriage equality. I later accepted the argument from many in the LGBTIQ community that the unnecessary public debate a plebiscite would prompt could harm vulnerable young people. In addition, I know from experience in 2010, when my government oversaw a conscience vote in the NSW Parliament on same-sex adoption, that MPs can and do manage such debates thoughtfully. Nonetheless, the idea of more plebiscites in Australia is worthwhile. The fact remains that the plebiscite on marriage equality gave power to the Australian people to take action after the Coalition refused to let the parliament do its job and legislate for same-sex marriage. Should Labor win the next election, we will take a plebiscite to the people to ask if Australia should become a republic.

While Denniss argues that neoliberalism is dead, he accepts that it may not yet be buried. There are some upcoming tests of its vitality.

For two years, the Coalition government has run a campaign to cut the corporate tax rate, arguing that the way to create "jobs and growth" is to give an $80 billion handout to business in the form of a corporate tax cut. The private sector will solve the problem, the government says, if we just give them a break on their taxes.

Unsurprisingly, the biggest cheerleader for the government's proposed corporate tax cut is the Business Council of Australia. Twice in the past year, I asked the BCA to name just one country in the world where cutting the corporate tax rate led to higher wages for workers. Twice it failed to answer the question.

Earlier this year in the United States, the Trump company tax cuts came into effect. What has happened in the months since? Wages and investment have declined. Dividends to shareholders and executive pay have increased. Consider Harley-Davidson: one month after the Trump tax cuts came into effect, Harley-Davidson shut a factory in Missouri, put 800 Americans out of work, spent $700 million on share buybacks, increased dividends to shareholders and announced it was opening a factory in Thailand.

My favourite critique of the Coalition government's proposed corporate tax cut comes from *The Australian*'s economics editor, Adam Creighton. In February 2018, he drew inspiration from the "underpants gnomes" in the satirical television cartoon *South Park* to ridicule the idea that cutting corporate tax rates leads to wage growth:

> These fictitious creatures had a shonky business plan: Phase 1 was "collect underpants," Phase 3 was "profits." But when pressed by the character Kyle about Phase 2, how the collected underpants would actually lead to profit, the gnomes couldn't explain but pressed on regardless.
>
> It's a bit like the government's plan to cut corporate tax. Phase 1 is cutting the company tax rate to 25 per cent by 2026 and Phase 3 is higher wages. Phase 2 is unclear. Is it "capital deepening" or "investment," or some sort of weird, unenforceable social contract that businesses will raise the wages of workers out of the goodness of their heart? Voters seem suspicious of all of them.

Australians know that economic inequality is widening. We see the scale of multinational tax avoidance. We are aware that wealthy people have access to rules and mechanisms to reduce their tax obligations. Middle- and low-income workers increasingly understand that tax cuts for the top end of town will not flow through to the average household budget. We don't need to hear the IMF assessment that trickle-down theory is discredited. We know, after years of listening to broken promises from the right wing of politics, that fairness doesn't trickle down.

Denniss points out that many Australians seem responsive to Labor's renewed focus on reducing economic inequality and investing in public services. Policies such as removing most dividend imputation cash refunds and limiting the use of family trusts to minimise tax obligations seem to resonate with the community, especially when such policies sit alongside increased public investment in health, education and infrastructure.

The next general election will be a referendum on these issues.

Kristina Keneally

DEAD RIGHT

Correspondence

Adam Creighton

"If Australia was ever a workers' paradise, it isn't anymore." Richard Denniss is among the nation's more thoughtful commentators, and his essay *Dead Right* entertainingly skewers some of the cant and hypocrisy that pervades public policy debate. But it exaggerates economic problems and offers tired solutions that would make inequality worse.

"Neoliberalism," which he defines as "the catch-all term for all things small government," has progressively seeped into every crevice of society over the past thirty years, Dennis contends, enriching corporate interests at the expense of public services.

But it hasn't: if anything, government spending and regulation have increased. If "neoliberalism" is to mean anything more than gouging, greed or "something we don't like," then it's a lack of it that is eroding confidence in the status quo.

As Denniss contends, free markets are a tool to lower prices and increase quality. When they work, they are brilliant: think food or cars. When they don't, rent-seeking ensues.

Denniss's essay makes several terrific points about how the simplistic application of free-market ideas, dressed up as a quest for "competitiveness" alongside tendentious "modelling," has sometimes led to poor outcomes for consumers. These points are marred, however, by a snarky style that seems to cast advocates of free markets as villains – without compassion for refugees, the unemployed or the disabled, for instance. "We wouldn't want to give sick people the wrong incentives, would we?" he writes sarcastically.

And by a few errors, perhaps owing to hasty research: most of the references are to newspaper articles. "[Australia] is a country full of busy, stressed and insecure people ... too busy to play footy, cricket or netball on the weekends," he writes, adding that Australians "work some of the longest hours in the developed world."

Yet Australia is still a paradise for workers, relatively, having among the highest minimum wages in the world. We work an average of just under thirty-six hours a week, or fewer than one-third of daylight hours – hardly drudgery. Mexicans, Turks and Colombians work more than forty-five, according to the OECD's figures.

Importantly, headlines about real wage growth don't paint the whole picture, because new and improved digital technology isn't being adequately factored into price indices, as Harvard's Martin Feldstein recently pointed out, which leaves growth in living standards looking tardier than it really is.

Denniss romanticises 1950s industrial laws, but I'd rather be an Australian worker today. GDP per person has increased 63 per cent since 1987 alone, he notes. Neoliberalism's supposed triumph has accompanied a dramatic improvement in quality of life for most people.

Cost-of-living pressures have been greatest for those goods and services subsidised, regulated or provided by government: education, health, child care. Government-owned central banks have kneecapped housing affordability by keeping interest rates artificially low.

Meanwhile, government spending continues to soak up more and more national income. As a share of GDP, it's increased from around 22 per cent at the end of the Whitlam government to 25 per cent today. The National Disability Insurance Scheme, which will cost more than $20 billion a year, is almost certain to see that ratio tick higher. Both major political parties are promising to increase income tax as a share of the economy, the Liberals a little more slowly.

Is this rampant neoliberalism?

In fact, Joseph Schumpeter's expectation that free-market economies would become sclerotic, bogged down by public and private bureaucracy, appears to be coming true as more and more of us work for government directly or indirectly, or for giant oligopolies that function similarly.

Denniss's proposals include a sovereign wealth fund and more government agencies, including a federal anti-corruption commission and a new "national interest commission," all alongside a new "charter of rights." These would be a certain boon for lawyers, the senior executive service and financiers, but not for ordinary people.

His proposal to increase the number of MPs is interesting. "The greater the distance between our politicians and ourselves, the greater the influence the media, lobbyists and party officials have," he notes.

The essay is strongest on the inconsistency of advocates for privatisation, who argue the state isn't competent to run a business but is somehow competent to regulate new profit and bonus-maximising owners. "You get exactly the same electrons out of exactly the same wires ... All the costs of marketing this essential service, and all the profits extracted by all the competitors, are passed on to consumers in the form of higher prices," Denniss says, referring to increasingly dysfunctional electricity markets.

A free market only works effectively when prices are salient, when customers understand the product or service as well as sellers, and when there are many of both.

As Denniss argues, these conditions are far from satisfied in many cases, such as electricity or financial services, which enjoy vast implicit subsidies and exhibit little genuine competition. Too often, policy-making in Australia has naively assumed well-meaning policies wouldn't be severely abused. Funding for vocational training springs to mind. This isn't neoliberalism so much as stupidity.

Pejorative labels don't help the critique much. The terms "left-wing" and "right-wing" are increasingly meaningless; society is divided more and more by insiders with connections and fat salaries sustained by various streams of economic rent – and everyone else.

Nevertheless, some of the blame for what Denniss decries must be sheeted home to those who put themselves in the former category. Identity politics has so consumed many on the left – with Denniss, it must be said, an honourable exception – that there's little time left to protect policy-making from those who would abuse Adam Smith quotes to further their own interests. Keeping prices down and quality up is the best way to help ordinary workers and the unemployed.

Adam Creighton

Correspondence

Danielle Wood

Richard Denniss's *Dead Right* offers a burning critique of neoliberalism and a call to arms for our leaders to focus on making the country – and not just the economy – better. The essay lands some powerful punches, but at times I was left wondering what it was that Richard was actually fighting. As an argument for demoting the central role of economics in policy debate and design, the essay does not convince. But as a case for reforming institutions to curb the worst excesses of vested interest influence over policy, it is compelling indeed.

Richard defines neoliberalism as "all things small government" and the idea that "market forces are superior to government decision-making." But he also slips in a very different concept: "the idea that's what's good for business is good for the country."

Richard's first definition of neoliberalism is all about competition and rugged individualism. It's an Ayn Randesque world where private firms duke it out in a Darwinian battle for survival and governments "get out of the way" by reducing taxes and regulation. His second definition is crony capitalism writ large, with firms extracting special deals from government and profits growing ever larger at the expense of workers, consumers and taxpayers. But the first doesn't have to imply the second.

He also draws out neoliberalism's human toll: less time for barbeques and netball games, more time at the office. Less money for helping kids with cancer but more for maintaining subsidies for the fossil-fuel industries. The reader might be forgiven for thinking that Richard has fallen into the well-worn trap of using "neoliberalism" to mean "anything I don't like." Certainly, it would be difficult to find anyone rushing proudly to declare themselves a neoliberal under Richard's broader definition.

But I – and I suspect many others – would be willing to be outed as what might be called "neoliberal lites." ("Social liberalism" might be another term for this position but, like "neoliberalism," it's used too vaguely to be helpful, meaning all things to all people.)

We lites generally favour competition and markets. Competition among private providers is in most cases the best way to deliver better and more innovative products, and lower prices for consumers. Richard concedes that markets generally work better than central allocation – even for him, the idea of a fixed supply of public servant baristas pulling middling cappuccinos is a bridge too far.

Certainly, our heavily regulated world before the market-based reforms of the 1980s and 1990s was no consumer paradise. People sometimes waited weeks for the Telecom monopoly to connect the phone. Unmarried women couldn't get home loans. Supermarkets closed by 4pm Monday to Friday and at noon on Saturdays.

But embracing competition is not the same as blind faith in market solutions or believing that we should "let the market rip" in all cases. The economist Oliver Hart won the Nobel Prize for highlighting the risks of "quality shading" when governments outsource public services. Private-sector operators might be more entrepreneurial, but some of their entrepreneurial spirit will be channelled into finding ways to cut costs and quality while remaining within the strict letter of their contract with government.

Neoliberal lites recognise that the risks of outsourcing to the private sector are much higher for services like aged care and child protection, where customers are vulnerable and it is difficult to specify and enforce service quality. Government or not-for-profit provision is almost always the right answer in sectors where poor service can risk lives or dignity and where monitoring costs are prohibitive. That a blind "private sector is best" mentality can lead to the terrible outcomes Richard compellingly documents would be no surprise to most economists.

Other markets require careful regulatory oversight. The privatisation of electricity poles and wires substantially lowered prices by reducing the gold plating and cost padding that occurred under government ownership. But flaws in the way the regulatory system was designed (including generous appeal rights and a naive Competition Tribunal) later saw prices head in the wrong direction. Ironically, the government-owned Queensland and NSW network providers proved the most rapacious exploiters of the system – a worthwhile reminder that government ownership is no panacea without well-designed regulation.

Richard's essay provides little insight into how we should decide when government provision is best and when and how to regulate.

Lites also believe that incentives matter in policy design. That doesn't mean we want to deny sick people health care or leave the jobless beneath the poverty line, as Richard claims. But it does mean recognising that all government decisions involve trade-offs. Governments can of course increase taxes to pay for more spending. But there's no way around the fact that increasing most taxes comes at a cost. Higher taxes mean people work less or save and invest less. Free lunches are not always as delicious as they might seem. The reason so many economists drone on about tax reform is because we want to raise money to pay for social services in the way that creates the smallest drag on the economy.

Neoliberal lites embrace a proper analysis of costs and benefits. Richard is right that we shouldn't ask technocrats to answer values questions. The size of government, how much we should redistribute income and the weight given to the interests of future generations are all issues for citizens and their elected representatives. But these values debates should not take place in an information vacuum.

The government is entitled to build inland rail or move the Pesticides and Veterinary Management Authority to Armidale, but surely citizens are entitled to know how much extra everyone else is paying for the promise of regional jobs in the (former) deputy prime minister's electorate. Cost-benefit analysis works as a policy-maker's Google Maps: it gives guidance on the best way to reach a destination and, importantly, the costs of deviating from the preferred route.

Richard claims that economic frameworks and language have narrowed the policy debate. Certainly, the constant (and sometimes content-free) calls to boost productivity are tiresome even for an economist. But the claim that economic reform advocates have convinced the media and the public that other debates are a distraction doesn't ring true. Social policy reformers have chalked up a number of recent wins: the Victorian government legalised voluntary euthanasia, the NSW government legalised medical marijuana, and the Commonwealth government legislated for same-sex marriage after 62 per cent of Australians voted "yes" in a postal ballot. All of these took place against the backdrop of a wide-ranging (and generally constructive) public debate.

The economic language and tools that Richard derides are probably the most useful defence against the very real public policy concerns he articulates in his essay. Lites would be in furious agreement about the corrosive effects on policy when vested interests run roughshod over the national interest.

Economists have long warned of the danger of crony capitalism and the wastefulness of rent-seeking where firms channel their efforts into pushing for special favours from government rather than providing better service to their customers. Richard's examples of coffee-cart-stifling cafe owners, militant pharmacists and overzealous patent protectors are but a few of the many business groups putting up their hands for more regulation where it suits their interests.

The Australian political system has proved a fertile ecosystem for rent-seekers. Australian political parties rely more heavily on private donations than those in most other developed nations. Lobby groups can pluck former ministers and their staff straight from office without any sanction. Outside of New South Wales, Queensland and the ACT, the public has no visibility over who meets with their elected representatives. While public servants can't accept so much as a cup of coffee from a business because of the perceived risk of a conflict of interest, most of our elected representatives are free to accept as many overseas trips or tickets to major sporting events as they wish.

It's no wonder Australians are cynical. More than half agree that government is run for a few big interests. And, according to the Australian Election Study 1987–2016, an alarming 74 per cent believe that people in government look after themselves. Richard is right that these perceptions of a rotten core contribute to a lack of trust in politicians and our system of government.

We can do more to blunt the power of vested interests in the political debate. A federal anti-corruption watchdog would help. So would restricting political expenditure to end the donations arms race, publishing ministerial diaries and enforcing waiting periods for ministers who want to move into lobbying roles. Boosting the advocacy capacity of smaller interest groups would reduce the undue influence of concentrated interests in much policy formation.

Ultimately, Richard's essay doesn't convince me that we need to throw the neoliberal market baby out with the crony capitalist bathwater. Promoting competition and harnessing market forces have generally served Australia well. Blind faith in markets and giving priority to vested interests over the national interest have not. By conflating the two, Richard misses the opportunity to show us how we can do economic policy better. And we need more economists of Richard's calibre doing just that.

Danielle Wood

DEAD RIGHT

Correspondence

Damien Freeman

One curious feature of Richard Denniss's critique of "neoliberalism" is that it seems to be calling for a decidedly conservative response. Denniss is concerned by the loss of trust in institutions, which he attributes to neoliberalism. It is interesting to identify the conservative nature of some of his concerns, and why a better understanding of conservative thought might shed some light on aspects of his critique.

Denniss suggests that the significance of the economic rationalists in the 1980s was that they "were putting a wider range of policies on the policy menu" but that, over time, "ideas of neoliberalism have been used to push all other options off that menu."

If one reads the account in Paul Kelly's *The End of Certainty*, what one finds is that the 1980s was more about responding to specific challenges than it was about creating a range of policy options. John Howard was prepared to support Bob Hawke and Paul Keating in addressing those specific challenges. It is true that this involved Howard's coming to identify himself increasingly as an economic liberal. But Denniss seems to forget that when Howard reflected on his political thought, he tended to say that he was both an economic liberal and a social conservative.

What Howard meant by labelling himself a social conservative was that he was committed to Edmund Burke's conception of society as formed by institutions: the constitution, parliament, the monarchy, the family, marriage, and organised (albeit not established) religion. Burkeans such as Howard say that society is possible because of the institutions through which people come together to affirm their shared values. These institutions enable people to form bonds of trust with other members of the institutions, precisely because they share their values, and to trust the institutions themselves because they affirm the shared values of a tradition. It is the loss of this trust that is one of the central themes of Denniss's analysis.

Denniss says that "one of the great ironies of neoliberalism is that even though it was supported by many conservative Christians … it rendered many Christians unable to live by traditional Christian values." Denniss's conception of "neoliberalism" may well be inconsistent with traditional Christian values, but that does not mean that every form of economic liberalism is incompatible with traditional morality.

Howard's two claims – that he was a social conservative and an economic liberal – were compatible because one could be committed to addressing the economic challenges of the 1980s through market reforms while retaining a commitment to the centrality of institutions for society. If "neoliberalism" is incompatible with a commitment to the central place of institutions in society, then Howard is evidently the kind of economic liberal who is not a "neoliberal."

British MP, minister and author of *Adam Smith: What He Thought and Why it Matters* Jesse Norman was in Sydney earlier this year to deliver the second P.M. Glynn Lecture on Religion, Law and Public Life. Norman explained that Adam Smith gives us the idea of commercial society, and that capitalism emerges as one version of commercial society. Capitalism is not the only form that commercial society can take, and the excesses of an extreme form of capitalism, to which the global financial crisis was witness, are an invitation to return to its roots in commercial society, and to consider what form of commercial society might be best for society today.

Norman points out that although some recent versions of capitalism might have abandoned any notion of morality, this is not true of commercial society. Smith understood commercial society to be predicated upon moral institutions, and Norman urges us to embrace forms of commercial society that take seriously the role of moral, social and political institutions, rather than some debased form of capitalism that sees no place for such institutions in our life in common.

One of the hallmarks of neoliberalism, according to Denniss, is that it gives primacy to the need "to 'grow our economy' some more" rather than the need "to rebuild trust in our institutions and confidence in our country." The obsession with economic growth seems to plague politicians on both sides of the political divide in Australia at the moment, so if this is a legacy of neoliberalism, it seems to have been bequeathed equally among the political class. However, the idea that the only way in which it is rational to discuss politics is in economic terms is not shared by all politicians.

It is particularly instructive to examine the way Tony Abbott writes about the Howard ministry's achievements and, indeed, its weaknesses. As I explain in my book *Abbott's Right*, Abbott maintained that, whatever the Howard ministry's successes were (and he was in no doubt about these), there had been a failure of communication – at least in its dying days. The leaders, he conceded, had failed to explain to the people that the economic policy they were advocating was directed towards social ends, rather than merely an economic end. Abbott is very clear that ultimately economic policy must be justified in terms of social outcomes. If neoliberals succumb to the fallacy that the only rational way to discuss public policy is in terms of economics, then Abbott's analysis is not neoliberal.

Denniss argues that neoliberalism has "stripped public debate of its intimate, personal and intangible characteristics." Any cursory reading of Jesse Norman's previous book, *Edmund Burke: Philosopher, Politician, Prophet*, will see that such "neoliberalism" bears no relation whatsoever to Burke's understanding of the role of emotion – or temper – in statesmanship. More than that, the politicians whom Denniss seems to identify most closely with neoliberalism are in fact better understood in the mould of Burkean political thought: in his heyday, no one doubted that Howard understood the temper of the Australian people and was responsive to their intimate, personal and intangible characteristics.

Denniss also writes that "according to the neoliberal view of the world, fear, like greed, is good," and cites Abbott's approach to unemployment as an example of the use that can be made of fear in policy-making. This entirely misrepresents Abbott's understanding of the dignity of work. He has a deep commitment to the importance of work, and this involves having regard for emotions such as fear and pride. Abbott believes that it is right that people take pride in providing for themselves and their families through the fruit of their labours, and it is natural that they should be afraid of losing this capacity. Burke tells us that leaders need to understand the way pride and fear operate among the people, if they want to be effective leaders of those people. This is not to glorify the role of fear in public life. It is to adopt an approach to public policy that is sensitive to the sources of fear and pride in people's working lives. It is not to glorify fear as a political tool.

By the end of the essay, it is still not clear what neoliberalism is, and so it is not clear whether this category is intended to capture all forms of commercial society, or only certain extreme versions of capitalism. Consequently, it is not clear who in the Australian political landscape is captured by Denniss's "neoliberalism." Whoever they are, they are not people who share Burke's commitment to social institutions or Smith's commitment to commercial society. There may be reasons to reject the politics of Howard and Abbott, but it is not because they are neoliberals. Indeed, they share some of the concerns that seem to motivate Denniss's critique of neoliberalism.

Denniss is dead right to warn us of the threat that a loss of trust in institutions poses for society. Implicit in his argument is that if we are concerned about what comes next, we need to return to the conservative tradition of Edmund Burke, which extols the importance of institutions, values and trust for society, and to Adam Smith's commercial society predicated on moral institutions, rather than squabbling about whether the responses to the economic challenges of the 1980s have left us with an unhelpful approach that might – with some difficulty – be classified as "neoliberal."

Damien Freeman

DEAD RIGHT | *Correspondence*

Michael Keating

I believe that Richard Denniss and I share the same values. We both want an inclusive society and think that such a society will not be achieved by relying purely on market forces. Instead, we see a continuing role for government intervention to achieve that inclusive society, and we think that this will require a modest future increase in government revenue. The future of capitalism and our democracy depends upon the success of governments in maintaining inclusive economic growth. Indeed, the failure of the governments of many advanced economies to maintain such growth throughout this century is most responsible for the swing to extreme right-wing populist governments – the principal challenge to the open, liberal international order.

Where Denniss and I part company is that Denniss blames all the faults he sees in modern society, some of which he exaggerates, on what he calls "neoliberalism." He is in good company. There are many other critics of neoliberalism, who blame it for everything they don't like about the direction our society and economy have taken over the last thirty-odd years.

The first problem that I have with these arguments is that typically neoliberalism is never explicitly defined. Its definition is inferred through its alleged impacts, without any regard for the logic of cause and effect. In fairness, Denniss is a bit better than this. He suggests that "Neoliberalism [is] the catch-all term for all things small government." But, as Denniss himself concedes, the size of government is bigger than ever, as measured by the amount of regulation, and government expenditure and revenue are both at an all-time high relative to GDP. So, if neoliberalism is defined by smaller government, while government is in fact bigger, by what logic is neoliberalism responsible for the ills afflicting society? However, Denniss also has another approach to defining neoliberalism, suggesting that "it is possible to think of neoliberalism as an ideology focused on the idea that market forces are superior to government decision-making."

Again, he provides no evidence to show that this ideology has dominated policy thinking in Australia.

Instead, I suggest that the micro-economic "reforms" introduced in the 1980s and 1990s, so often referred to as neoliberalism, involved:

- floating the Australian dollar
- financial deregulation and (later) changing the type of regulation
- largely eliminating protection, and a shift in industry assistance in favour of more generic assistance and less specific industry assistance
- tax reform to make the system more efficient and fair, but not to reduce the total revenue
- decentralising wage determination in favour of more enterprise bargaining
- some measure of privatisation accompanied by the introduction of competition policy.

These reforms can be broadly characterised as making greater use of markets, but Denniss doesn't really try to and I doubt that he could make the case that these reforms are directly responsible for the many aspects of today's society that he decries. The fundamental reason for many of these reforms was that the previous regulations were not working. For example, the previous attempts to "manage" the Australian currency were proving counterproductive, signalling the likely next movement to the speculators, and giving them a one-way bet. Similarly, protectionism wasn't working. These sorts of regulatory changes did not involve any attempt to reduce government responsibilities, as implied by the critics of neoliberalism. Rather, they represented an effort to improve the effectiveness of government intervention, as governments found that often they would be more effective if they focused more on *managing* markets and creating the right incentives and disincentives, and relied less on administrative controls that were increasingly being evaded or proving unworkable. Today, the equivalent approach would be to price carbon as the best way to reduce carbon emissions, rather than relying on direct action policies; it is curious that this reliance on pricing carbon has been supported by many of the critics of neoliberalism.

Privatisation and contracting out

My sense is that it may be privatisation that causes most of the disquiet about neoliberalism. There are, however, a few points to be made. First, the majority of economists long ago concluded that competition was a much more important determinant of corporate performance than ownership. Furthermore, the previous government ownership of commercial entities such as airlines and banks did not seem to be achieving any social purpose, with the government-owned airlines and banks behaving and having to behave in much the same way as their competitors to survive. Denniss himself agrees that whether a business should be publicly or privately owned should be considered on a case-by-case basis. I also agree with him that the case for privatising natural monopolies is much more difficult to sustain: governments must be confident that they can achieve the same outcomes or better by regulation than they can achieve by ownership and direct control.

However, Denniss has a particular beef about electricity that is worth exploring a little further. He claims that electricity privatisation has "cost Australian energy users billions of dollars" as "a privately owned monopoly [is] willing to spend millions of dollars to bamboozle the regulator." The chair of the Australian Competition and Consumer Commission (ACCC), Rod Sims, also agrees that "Australians are paying considerably more for electricity than they should." However, in its recent exhaustive review, the ACCC never mentioned privatisation, and Sims in a press conference made it clear that privatisation was not a cause of high electricity prices. The most damaging criticism made by Sims was that "some states, with the excellent exception of Victoria, often privatised generation and retail assets without an eye to competition, and mainly to maximise sale proceeds." Furthermore, the one period when electricity prices did stabilise was between 1993 and 2000, and this was when much of the privatisation actually occurred and when competition policy was introduced. In fact, as the Productivity Commission established in a review of the impact of National Competition Policy, "Before NCP and related reforms, it was widely recognised that electricity production and distribution activities were working well below best practice." So competition policy and privatisation did realise major productivity gains that were passed on in lower prices, although these were largely one-off gains and cannot be repeated. Finally, I think experience suggests that the public providers find it easier to raise capital for dubious investments; for example, if the Liddell power station were still in public hands, does anyone think the present government would agree to close it when it becomes uneconomic in a couple of years?

Privatisation was not always carried out well, but neither has it proved to be the disaster that many of its critics assert it to be.

I have already mentioned the limits placed on competition by some states as they tried to maximise the proceeds from sale of their electricity assets. Similarly, Denniss rightly criticises the restrictions on competition that accompanied the sale of the ports in New South Wales, but those restrictions would never have been endorsed if neoliberal policies had been followed. On the other hand, the major privatisations carried out by the Australian government – airlines, telecommunications and banking – did first establish a competitive environment before the sale, even though this then depressed the sale price.

My major criticism of deregulation and privatisation is that too often the required new regulatory regime was insufficiently thought through in advance. For example, it was only after the almost-failure of a major bank in the 1991 recession that the prudential regulation system was appropriately tightened up. Similarly, in the case of vocational education and training, significant gains were made in efficiency and in moving to a more responsive system for disadvantaged people by allowing them greater choice. Yet too often the quality of the vocational education and training was very unsatisfactory because insufficient effort was made to restrict access to public funding to only those private providers who had a track record of quality.

The case for and against contracting out is similar to privatisation. For example, a long time ago – well before the advent of neoliberalism – governments started contracting out construction activity, such as road building – and this seems to have received community-wide acceptance. Similarly, the community has long supported the system whereby medical services are mostly provided by private doctors who are then reimbursed totally or partially by the state. What may be more controversial is the contracting out of decisions that in the end affect the nature of government programs. For example, the Keating government in its One Nation package of assistance to long-term unemployed people decided to contract out the provision of employment and training advice and assistance. The reason was that although the former Commonwealth Employment Service had a reasonable record of assisting the typical job seeker, its culture was built around the provision of the *same uniform* service to all its clients, whereas long-term unemployed people required more individual assistance, which non-government providers were better at delivering.

However, I question the increasing contracting out of the analytical and advisory functions of the public service. Evaluation of policies and programs should be the foundation for much policy advice, and if the public service contracts out this function, then it is no wonder that its capacity to provide sound policy advice has atrophied. In addition, too often the use of a commercial consultancy firm results in the government getting the sort of analysis and advice that it wants to receive rather than frank and fearless advice, as the consultant wants to please in order to gain another contract.

Has neoliberalism changed the nature of politics?

Denniss's critique of neoliberalism is broader than the issues discussed so far. He decries what he sees as "the trick of neoliberalism": "to convince the public that it is the economic dimension of big issues that we must always focus on." In his view, neoliberalism "has been the ideal cloak behind which to conceal enormous shifts in Australia's wealth and culture. It has provided powerful people with the perfect language in which to dress up their self-interest as the national interest"; "it has radically altered the way we see the role of government"; and in relation to health care, "it has also hardened the hearts of average Australians towards those most in need."

This critique of neoliberalism has been made by others as well, although not always so eloquently. However, there is quite a lot of exaggeration in the evidence provided; and where the evidence is correct, the analysis does not really establish cause and effect, and alternative explanations are more probable.

Exaggerated evidence

For reasons of space, I will only give one example of exaggerated evidence, but there are others. Denniss says that all children with cancer should receive high-quality treatment, and then implies that our health system is too cruel to guarantee this. But this is quite false – these children *do* receive high-quality treatment, irrespective of their parents' means. Furthermore, every other week more very expensive drugs are added to the pharmaceutical benefits list once they have been assessed as safe and effective, and, while the amount of co-payments may be debatable, I am yet to see the evidence that anyone who is seriously ill (say, with cancer) is missing out on necessary treatment.

More generally in his discussion of access to health care, Denniss provides no evidence allowing us to make a proper comparison with the past, but he nevertheless concludes that there has been a massive deterioration. Thus, he cites approvingly Menzies' support for universal health care, but no one had more time to introduce such a system than Menzies, and he didn't. Of course, the reality is that the original system of universal health insurance was introduced by the Labor Whitlam government, then abandoned by the conservative Fraser government, which had nothing to do with neoliberalism, while the present Medicare system was introduced by the Hawke government, which was also responsible for embracing the policies that are cited as representing neoliberalism.

Denniss also fails to mention that Australia today has a world-class health system, which the Harvard-based health research institution the Commonwealth Fund has ranked second of eleven first-world countries. I agree with Denniss that there could be improvements to the effectiveness and equity of health care in Australia, but typically more could always be spent on almost all public and private services if the money were available. A more balanced assessment would have acknowledged that the rate of bulk-billing has been maintained, and over the last two decades public expenditure on health has increased faster than GDP.

The logic of cause and effect

Inequality has increased since the early 1980s in almost all the advanced economies, although rather less in Australia than most others. Interestingly, according to OECD data the biggest increases in inequality between 1985 and 2014 have been in Sweden and the United States, followed by New Zealand, Finland and Germany – and of course Sweden, Finland and Germany are not notable for their embrace of neoliberal policies. Instead, there is widespread agreement that the major cause of increasing inequality has been technological change, which has "hollowed out" middle-level jobs and has also tended to be skill-biased. In short, the adoption of neoliberal policies, to the extent that it has occurred, has little or nothing to do with the increase in inequality.

Similarly, it is not hard to think of a host of other reasons why we are more individualistic and have less trust in government, instead of adopting Denniss's hypothesis that these changes are all the fault of neoliberalism. Society has become more individualistic, which predates neoliberal policies. Key drivers are increased education, which has helped create citizens who are more critical of authority, but also more tolerant of individual differences; women have more independence; the car, television and the internet have increased people's choices and people now feel they have the capacity to live as they choose and the right to do so. Well before the advent of neoliberalism, increasing living standards and modern technologies were also changing lifestyles; marriage break-up has become much more common, most of us no longer travel together on public transport, and our leisure time is more likely to be spent watching TV or a video, or using the internet, rather than engaging in community activities or even group activities in the home. With fewer opportunities for face-to-face contact with other people, it is not surprising that we have become more individualistic.

The loss of trust in government is also not a new phenomenon; many writers analysed it more than twenty years ago. According to Jane Mansbridge, it is the incapacity of governments to meet the different and typically incompatible expectations of different groups of citizens over a wide range of issues that are inherently insoluble that is most responsible for the decline in trust in government. In addition, in this century economic stagnation has meant that governments no longer meet the popular expectation that living standards will improve over time. Many people feel that they and their government have lost control over their destiny, and with that there is a tendency for governments to lose authority and trust. Perhaps not surprisingly, the people who feel most disempowered are those who have fallen behind economically. But whether these disempowered people have lost faith in government or faith in the elites whom they see as dominating government is a moot point.

Conclusion

Denniss states the curious opinion that "there has been no obsession among the political elite with the neoliberal goals of reducing government spending, regulation or tax collection over the past three decades." But I don't think that neoliberalism demands adherence to specific goals. Denniss also writes that "Paul Keating and former NSW premier Bob Carr were two prominent examples of a generation of ALP figures who passionately embraced some of the key tenets of neoliberalism, albeit in parallel with a strong welfare safety net and social wage." As someone who worked closely with Paul Keating when he was prime minister, I have no doubt that he remained totally committed to traditional Labor goals, but he recognised that the best means of achieving them had to change with the times.

Denniss's critique of neoliberalism presumes that it is some sort of government *objective*, in its own right. If that were true, it might be possible to argue that neoliberalism is to at least some extent responsible for the outcomes achieved. However, neoliberalism was never an objective of policy, nor strategy. Instead, improving markets is seen as a *means* to better achieve traditional government objectives.

Most importantly, policies described as neoliberal have aimed to improve the competitiveness and flexibility of Australian markets, and thanks to their success in this regard, Australia has managed to experience twenty-seven years of unbroken economic growth, something that Denniss fails to acknowledge in his critique. And although Denniss is no fan of improvements in material living standards, many Australian families say that they are struggling to meet their costs of living, and without this long period of growth, unemployment would be significantly higher.

Nor do I think that neoliberalism has had any major unintended consequences for our values. Australia remains a most egalitarian country. Our tax-transfer system is so highly targeted that it achieves more distribution than any other country in the world. It is true that conservatives support less redistribution than Labor, but that has always been the case, and even the conservatives have never radically changed the amount of redistribution achieved.

The so-called reform agenda of the current government and its business supporters, with its focus on tax cuts and reducing protections for workers, is not at all new. In fact, the acts of parliament covering taxation and industrial relations are the two most-amended pieces of legislation since Federation. What we are really seeing is the traditional conflict between labour and capital being played out in not very different ways.

Although it is easy to be critical of the present government's agenda, or more accurately its lack of any agenda, that cannot realistically be attributed to neoliberalism. Instead, this government has allowed itself to become beholden to a very traditional set of conservative interests. These interests have nothing to do with neoliberal policies; indeed, these backwoods conservatives are usually opposed to any liberal policies and are only interested in promoting their own vested interests and finding scapegoats for anything that goes wrong.

Michael Keating

Roderick Best

In developing a critique of the surviving rhetoric of "economic rationalism," Richard Denniss used two examples to put into stark relief the consequences of economic practices upon the lives of two people to justify his title *Dead Right*. I do not know the background to the very sad circumstances surrounding the death of Shirley Carter, but I am aware of the circumstances surrounding the death of the young child, Braxton Slager. I was present every day at, and gave evidence in, the coronial inquiry into Braxton's death.

Braxton was a bright and energetic three-year-old boy who tragically died. We absolutely do need to learn from his death. What we need to learn is how better to look after children in state care. What is not helpful, however, is when the apparent example does not in fact justify the assertion. In those circumstances we lose focus. The argument is weakened and the death of a child becomes a footnote, rather than producing a change in how we care for children.

The coroner's decision was clear that Braxton entered a short-term care arrangement because neither of his parents could provide the immediate care necessary to look after him. This was *not* a removal of a child by the state. The arrangement for his care was *not* part of the program Denniss describes: "in the name of efficiency the Department of Family and Community Services had 'outsourced' the role of finding suitable homes for vulnerable children many years ago." During the short period this arrangement was in place, the department, at all times, retained responsibility for the care of Braxton. The circumstances of Braxton's death are not related to the failures of neoliberalism that are central to Denniss's argument.

The tragedy of Braxton's death should not be cheapened by using it as a pop-up illustration for a discussion of "enormous shifts in Australia's wealth and culture" – no matter how important that discussion might be. For matters of worth to come from personal tragedy, the respectful approach is to focus on the tangible, practical matters that will help other children have better lives. What these changes should be are encapsulated in the recommendations made by the coroner after a comprehensive and exhaustive consideration of what happened to Braxton. It is telling that none of the four recommendations from the coroner addressed deficiencies in the new model of outsourcing foster care. These changes applied equally to practice before the changes commenced. The recommendations looked at the emotional and psychological supports provided to carers who were no longer looking after a foster child who had formed part of their family for a number of years; how policies that were put in place, not for cost-cutting and efficiency but for the care of the child, needed to better address the child's needs; and the role of the state department in ensuring the suitability of accommodation when it had ongoing responsibility for the child. Life Without Barriers is making the relevant changes applicable to its practice.

Honouring the tragic death of the vulnerable in our society requires us to honestly and respectfully consider what happened and then make real, verifiable changes in response. It is not about misconstruing what happened so as to apply a theory, out of context, to advance a different argument.

Roderick Best

DEAD RIGHT

Response to Correspondence

Richard Denniss

For Grant, who personifies the best of Australian values.

As theologians know, it's hard to write clearly about something that may not exist. Likewise, as an economist, I found it very hard to write about an idea that, while widely discussed, seemingly has no actual advocates in Australia. So why write an essay about neoliberalism if no one promotes it, I hear you ask. Simple: monsters don't have to exist to scare children, gods don't have to exist to give people comfort, and the fact no politicians admit to being racist doesn't mean that racism isn't a powerful idea in Australia. Similarly, that no federal politician declares himself or herself a neoliberal doesn't mean neoliberalism isn't a powerful rhetorical and political idea.

For a writer, there is nothing more frustrating than a reader who completely misses your point. Is it me? Is it them? Is it the limits of language? How could someone read so many of my words and miss my point so completely? In turn, the most frustrating critical responses to my essay were those that seemed to agree entirely with my main point without realising this. Clearly I need to improve my communication skills.

First of all, I thank the respondents for taking the time not just to read my essay, but to comment on it. As Oscar Wilde quipped, the only thing worse than being talked about is not being talked about. I am grateful and flattered that such a range of thinkers gave their time to discuss my essay.

John McTernan clearly didn't like it. But while his response makes clear that he read my words carefully, it's hard for me to understand how he failed to grasp their meaning. The whole point of my essay is to say that among modern Australian politicians, not one consistently relies on neoliberal principles to guide their words or deeds. Not one. As evidence for this, I point out that Matt Canavan (an ex–Productivity Commission economist) now wants to subsidise coalmines; that

Tony Abbott (the man who gave us the Commission of Audit) now wants to nationalise coalfired power stations; and that the premier of New South Wales, Gladys Berejiklian (once renowned as a fan of privatisation), now wants to nationalise football stadiums. I thought it was important to show the way conservative politicians and business leaders lean on "neoliberal principles" when they want to explain their desire to cut welfare spending, but abandon these same "principles" when they feel like subsidising powerful industries such as mining and private education. Alas, it seems some of my respondents thought that this point didn't really need making. I still do.

McTernan's critique of my argument includes the observation that neither Tony Abbott nor John Howard was really a neoliberal because they actually supported government intervention when they felt like it. Yep. That's exactly the point I was trying to make on page 1 of the essay. Similarly, in his response Damien Freeman agrees with McTernan that neither Howard nor Abbott was a neoliberal. Again, I can only agree. They weren't. They were clever politicians who hunted with the neoliberal foxes when they felt like it and ran with the populist hounds when it was in their political interest to do so. (Damn, why didn't I write that sentence so clearly in the essay?)

The most common criticism of the responses is that I didn't clearly and consistently define what I meant by neoliberalism. I tried. I defined it on page 1 as "the catch-all term for all things small government, [which] has been the ideal cloak behind which to conceal enormous shifts in Australia's wealth and culture." I went on to say that:

> It has provided powerful people with the perfect language in which to dress up their self-interest as the national interest. Without such a cloak, policies to slash income support for those most in need while giving tax cuts to those with the most money would just look nasty … the purpose of this essay is to consider, in the age of Trump, Brexit and Pauline Hanson 2.0, how the neoliberal agenda of "free markets," "free trade" and "trickle-down tax cuts" has wounded our national identity, bled our national confidence, caused paralysis in our parliaments, and is eating away at the identity of those on the right of Australian politics.

Perhaps I was being too subtle, but what I was trying to say, at the very beginning of the essay, was that the term "neoliberalism" is primarily a rhetorical device used to conceal the underlying motivations of politicians who, for example, want to cut spending on public schools and increase subsidies for private schools without having to reveal their personal desire to do so.

The reason I quoted the mother of neoliberalism, Margaret Thatcher, saying that "Economics are the method; the object is to change the heart and soul," was to shift the way neoliberalism is examined. For decades, economists, social policy experts and citizens have debated issues such as whether privatising health leads to better outcomes at lower cost or worse ones at higher cost. But such debates have done little to dampen enthusiasm for privatisation among those in power (in both major parties). In my essay, I set out instead to explore the rhetorical and policy contradictions of those who sometimes push so hard for the neoliberal agenda of free markets, free trade and trickle-down economics.

Just as the desire of postwar Britons to pull together and invest in national health and welfare systems irritated Margaret Thatcher, my distinction between what neoliberalism says it is and what neoliberal rhetoric has been used to do clearly irritated McTernan, who points out that I inconsistently use the term more than one hundred times in the essay. I'm not sure that I do, but let me try to find common ground. I think there is a big difference between what neoliberalism is and what neoliberalism has done. Of the twelve different "definitions" that McTernan thinks I used, they fit pretty neatly into two groups.

The first group of definitions covers the underlying beliefs of neoliberalism, all of which I think are covered by my "catch-all" definition.

- small government
- outsourcing public services
- the profit motive
- measuring efficiency and quality
- reducing the budget deficit and public spending
- cutting regulation
- the idea that market forces are superior to government decision-making.

And the second group of "definitions" he says that I use are, I think, better seen as the cultural consequences of decades of inculcation in neoliberal beliefs about human nature and economics. These include:

- sponsorship of museums
- looking out for yourself
- the last thirty years of Australian government
- cultural change of hearts and minds
- the assertion "there is no alternative."

While I'm glad I peppered the essay with different examples, I do sympathise with McTernan's confusion. Abbott thinks that the tobacco taxes he increased while health minister were a good way to reduce smoking and that carbon taxes were a terrible way to reduce greenhouse-gas emissions. Abbott's Commission of Audit was unambiguously based on the "principle" that reducing government spending was good for the economy, yet as prime minister he championed an enormously expensive paid-parental-leave scheme. It's hard to write consistently about such inconsistent principles.

But again, I'd like to thank McTernan for helping me to clarify my point. In short, for the avoidance of any doubt, I didn't mean to suggest that museum sponsorship is the definition of neoliberalism, but I very much meant to say that neoliberal rhetoric has played a central role in making a country as rich as Australia feel so poor that we need to use our National War Memorial to promote the logos of weapons manufacturers more visibly than we remember those individuals who died fighting for our country. I think the symbolism of war memorials is extremely important, but then again I think national identity is a very important, and contestable, concept. McTernan, on the other hand, thinks that national identity is "an inverted pyramid of piffle," so perhaps it's little wonder he doesn't share my concern with the way that neoliberalism has been used to transform Australia's identity.

I was happy to take the bitter medicine doled out by some respondents, but I was even happier that there was so much substantive and insightful analysis and critique to chew on. Adam Creighton, for example, shares my frustration with the lack of honesty that underpins what should be important economic and democratic debates about the relative size of the public sector in Australia and the best way to regulate private companies. Having accepted my definition of neoliberalism (phew), Creighton rejects my view that over the past thirty years neoliberalism has infected all corners of Australian life, and argues that, "if anything, government spending and regulation have increased. If 'neoliberalism' is to mean anything more than gouging, greed or 'something we don't like,' then it's a lack of it that is eroding confidence in the status quo." I agree with him entirely. If we had a greater focus on small government and the efficient use of public money, there is no way the current government would be trying to spend $1 billion subsidising the Adani coalmine. No way it would have offered a $454 million grant to a small charity set up by a group of businesspeople without any tender process. And there is no way that we would have privatised the vocational education and training sector at enormous cost to taxpayers, students and employers alike.

Similarly, I agree with Creighton when he writes,

> Meanwhile, government spending continues to soak up more and more national income. As a share of GDP, it's increased from around 22 per cent at the end of the Whitlam government to 25 per cent today. The National Disability Insurance Scheme, which will cost more than $20 billion a year, is almost certain to see that that ratio tick higher. Both major political parties are promising to increase income tax as a share of the economy, the Liberals a little more slowly. Is this rampant neoliberalism?

Again, the confusion stems from the difference between the stated objectives of neoliberals and the actual behaviour of successive governments, which have told the public they have "no choice" but to cut spending on services and "no choice" but to reduce the regulation of the finance sector at the very same time they choose to spend a lot more money subsiding the fossil-fuel industry and introducing a lot more regulation of unions, charities and the unemployed.

Creighton is a respected economics writer who works for one of the more conservative of our broadsheet newspapers. His views are neither radical nor ill-considered and, in turn, it's important that Australians of all political persuasions read his views about the role of the market carefully:

> A free market only works effectively when prices are salient, when customers understand the product or service as well as sellers, and when there are many of both …
>
> [T]hese conditions are far from satisfied in many cases, such as electricity or financial services, which enjoy vast implicit subsidies and exhibit little genuine competition. Too often, policy-making in Australia has naively assumed well-meaning policies wouldn't be severely abused. Funding for vocational training springs to mind. This isn't neoliberalism so much as stupidity.

Hear, hear. As someone who has lectured in economics for more than twenty years, I never cease to be amazed at how many people embark on an economics degree thinking that they have to "pick a team" and barrack for "free markets" or "red tape and regulation." The rhetoric of neoliberalism has debased the language of public debate so comprehensively that calls for regulation are quickly labelled "creeping socialism" and efforts to reduce government waste are described as "heartless." If only people like Adam and me could have such a debate without anyone calling either of us silly names.

As the head of the Department of Prime Minister and Cabinet from 1991 to 1996, Mike Keating is far better placed than me to speak on the objectives of, and options considered by, prime ministers Hawke and Keating. Although he starts his response by stating that he shares my values, he takes issue with my depiction of the motivation for and effectiveness of a wide range of neoliberal policies. While I didn't attempt to write the history of neoliberalism in Australia in the Hawke/Keating years, I do agree with Mike Keating that some neoliberal policies delivered some significant benefits to some groups in Australia. I thought I made clear that I supported some of them; as I said in the essay, I think the privatisation of Qantas was good for travellers and good for the budget.

While Keating and I clearly agree on many things, I reject his criticism that I exaggerate evidence of the impact of neoliberalism on our culture. In building his case, he cites but one example: "Denniss correctly considers that all children with cancer should receive high-quality treatment, and then implies that our health system is too mean to guarantee this. But this is quite false – these children do receive high-quality treatment irrespective of their parents' means." But I made no such claim. On the contrary, I simply posed the democratic question and explained that different democracies made different decisions:

> Should all children with cancer receive high-quality treatment, or only those whose parents can afford it? Should all adults with cancer receive the highest level of care, or only those who have the most expensive insurance? Different people in different countries come up with quite different answers to these questions. Not even Barack Obama suggested that all US citizens should have universal access to high-quality health care, and not even Tony Abbott suggested that Australia's publicly funded Medicare system should be removed.

I didn't say, or even imply, that Australia didn't help children with cancer. I simply used the question to highlight the fundamentally human nature of what are often depicted as "economic questions" about issues as complicated as the design of pharmaceutical subsidies. That said, a quick Google search would confirm for Keating that Australians who want access to certain drugs often decide to travel abroad and spend their life savings to obtain such treatments.

Other respondents raised specific concerns. Creighton, for example, was critical of my claim that Australia is no longer a "workers' paradise," even though today more than half of Australian workers no longer have access to paid holidays. While I don't disagree with his statement that he would rather be a worker today than in the 1950s, and I don't disagree that Australians work far fewer hours than the average Turk, Mexican or Colombian, I don't share his overall assessment of the state of our labour market. While labour-market data is relatively objective, it seems the definition of paradise, and the countries we wish to compare ourselves to, are in the eye of the beholder.

Without doubt, the criticism that stung most was the suggestion by Roderick Best that, "The tragedy of Braxton's death should not be cheapened by using it as a pop-up illustration for a discussion of 'enormous shifts in Australia's wealth and culture.'" Before including the example of the tragic death of Braxton Slager in my essay, I read the coroner's report into his death carefully. While Creighton criticises me for relying on newspapers for the claims made in the essay, they were by no means the only sources I relied on. I did, however, choose to reference easily accessible sources to help make the point that my critique of neoliberalism can be easily checked, and indeed extended upon, by any reader with access to the internet and a keen eye for contradiction. Yet no matter how carefully a researcher conducts their research, we all harbour the fear that the permanent written record of our thoughts might be in error, so it was with trepidation that I reread the coroner's report. On second reading, I think I pressed too gently on the role of neoliberalism. The NSW deputy coroner, Harriet Grahame, was damning of the process that led to the death:

> the rushed nature of this whole process [finding accommodation for a two-year-old], once it finally happened, meant that there was no chance to properly consider the appropriateness of where Braxton was to be placed. Given that FACS [NSW Family and Community Services] had been aware of the potential risks in Braxton's life since the first prenatal reports, it is disappointing that so little time and care went into this life changing decision ... There was no physical inspection of the premises and certainly no record of any discussion with the out of home carers about what to expect, prior to "dropping off" Braxton ... Even leaving aside the state of the premises, there were a number of factors which, if properly considered, should have indicated potential risk. Each of these factors should have been known to LWB [Life Without Barriers] during the assessment procedure ...
>
> In my view, the risk assessment procedure which took place was not a genuine assessment and is more accurately described as a rubber stamp given to a decision which had effectively already been made based on a lack of other options ... Mr Best, the State Director of LWB

> for NSW and the ACT, agreed in evidence that the state of the backyard, as depicted in photographs taken on the day of Braxton's death, was "alarming" and contained "many, many really obvious dangers for small children" ... the information systems operating at that time within LWB contributed to the poor understanding of the environment in which Braxton was to be placed ... The premises [his carer] could provide at that time were unsafe, and this should have been picked up by LWB ... Tragically, a child who went into care to improve his chance of living in a safe environment, found himself in a situation of enormous risk. His death appears to have been a preventable accident, which occurred against a background of inadequate care.

The coroner's report into the death of Braxton Slager is as gut-wrenching as it is damning of structural and systemic errors. But despite the content and the tone of the report, Best asserts in his response: "It is telling that none of the four recommendations from the coroner addressed deficiencies seen in the new model of outsourcing foster care." And he concludes: "Honouring the tragic death of the vulnerable in our society requires us to honestly and respectfully consider what happened and then make real, verifiable changes in response. It is not about misconstruing what happened so as to apply a theory, out of context, to advance a different argument."

While Best is correct that the coroner didn't make recommendations about "the new model of outsourcing foster care," few readers would likely realise that this silence says nothing, because by the time of the coronial inquiry both the NSW government and Best's organisation had made significant changes designed to reduce the risk faced by children in emergency care. In the words of the coroner: "I accept Counsel assisting's submission that there is no need for a formal recommendation pursuant to section 82 of the *Coroners Act* to provide a further catalyst for the reforms already identified. I accept a number of significant changes have already been made."

The most depressing element of the coroner's report, however, relates directly to the point of my essay (and the point rejected by Keating): that although Australia is one of the richest countries in the world, our governments frequently cite a shortage of funds as explanation for the low-quality services we often provide. The coroner recommended that greater psychological support be offered to those entrusted to care for vulnerable children, but "[t]he recommendation was not supported by FACS and LWB. Both were concerned by the potential expense." As I wrote in my essay:

> Mistakes and mistreatment in institutions are neither new nor entirely the fault of neoliberalism, but placing the profit motive at the heart of the delivery of care for the vulnerable creates a strong incentive to cut costs in an environment where customers are poorly placed to speak up for themselves, and at times literally incapable of it.

Braxton's tragic death is a sad indictment of the choices, and priorities, of successive governments and organisations involved in the care of the most vulnerable people in our community. The fact that Roderick Best cannot see that the culture of cost-cutting and "reducing red tape" played a central role in creating a system where there was no money to support carers and not enough "red tape" to ensure that houses were inspected before two-year-olds were "dropped off" is sadder still.

Max Corden and John Quiggin not only are two of the best economists Australia has produced, but they have also spent their lives applying their knowledge to the practical policy problems our country faces. While both gave me plenty to think about, the fact that such luminaries thought the topic of neoliberalism warranted careful examination, and that my take on it added a fresh dimension, is gratifying. Kristina Keneally's response contains a number of gems for my stump speech. Not only has she reminded me that the Business Council of Australia had been unable to provide her with a single example of a country where wage growth improved after a cut in the corporate tax rate, her US heritage prompts her to highlight the importance of our Australian Electoral Commission, whose independence is all that stands between us and the rampant gerrymandering on which American "democracy" is built. And I will be forever in her debt for alerting me to the fact that Adam Creighton and I share a propensity to use *South Park* episodes to make important points about the economy.

It is a privilege to have my arguments tested by such diverse voices. The conclusion of *Dead Right* is that the opposite of neoliberal economics isn't progressive economics, but engaged democracy. And engaged democracy requires exactly the sort of well-meaning debate contained in these pages. While it's inevitable that 25 million Australians will find it difficult to agree on priorities and policies, history suggests that good intentions and rigorous debate can move us forward, eventually. Our differences need not define us. Indeed, as the prime minister for whom John McTernan was head of communications once said, "We are us." Like the definition of neoliberalism, it's not quite clear what the phrase means, but that doesn't mean we shouldn't keep talking about it.

Richard Denniss

Roderick Best is state director of Life Without Barriers, NSW/ACT. He has worked in child protection for over thirty years, including as the inaugural General Counsel, Royal Commission into Institutional Responses to Child Sexual Abuse.

W. Max Corden is emeritus professor of international economics at Johns Hopkins University and has been a professorial fellow in the economics department of the University of Melbourne since 2002. He has been on the staff of the International Monetary Fund and a consultant for the World Bank. His most recent book is his autobiography, *Lucky Boy in the Lucky Country*.

Adam Creighton is economics editor of *The Australian*. He started his career at the Reserve Bank of Australia and studied economics at Oxford, where he was a Commonwealth Scholar.

Richard Denniss is chief economist at the Australia Institute. He writes for *The Monthly*, *The Canberra Times* and *The Australian Financial Review*. His books include *Curing Affluenza*, *Econobabble* and (as co-author) *Affluenza*.

Damien Freeman is a writer, lawyer and philosopher. He is the author of *Abbott's Right: The Conservative Tradition from Menzies to Abbott* and co-editor of *The Forgotten People: Liberal and Conservative Approaches to Recognising Indigenous Peoples*.

Michael Keating is a former head of the Australian Public Service and between 1983 and 1996 was secretary of the departments of Employment and Industrial Relations, Finance and Prime Minister and Cabinet. A visiting fellow at ANU, he is co-author of *Fair Share: Competing Claims and Australia's Economic Future*, published earlier this year.

Kristina Keneally is a federal Labor senator and was premier of New South Wales between 2009 and 2011.

John McTernan is a British political strategist and commentator. He was UK prime minister Tony Blair's director of political operations from 2005 to 2007, and director of communications for Prime Minister Julia Gillard from September 2011 to June 2013.

John Quiggin is an Australian Laureate Fellow in economics at the University of Queensland and the author of *Zombie Economics*. His blog, at johnquiggin.com, presents commentary from a social-democratic viewpoint.

Laura Tingle is chief political correspondent for ABC TV's 7.30. She won the Paul Lyneham Award for Excellence in Press Gallery Journalism in 2004, and Walkley Awards in 2005 and 2011. She is the author of *Chasing the Future: Recession, Recovery and the New Politics in Australia* and two previous acclaimed Quarterly Essays, *Great Expectations* and *Political Amnesia*.

Danielle Wood is director of the Budget Policy and Institutional Reform program at the Grattan Institute. Previously, she worked at the Australian Competition and Consumer Commission as the principal economist and director of merger investigations and as a senior research economist at the Productivity Commission.

www.ingramcontent.com/pod-product-compliance
Ingram Content Group UK Ltd.
Pitfield, Milton Keynes, MK11 3LW, UK
UKHW051206260726
13967UKWH00011B/3133